T0199149

# ADVANCED REVIEWS

*All through Christ: Christ through All* is another inspiring book by Dr. Yvette Hickman. She writes as a practicing physician and a committed Christian woman. She so passionately points out that we need Jesus in all of life's endeavors. She lets us know that Jesus Christ is the help that we need and the help that's available to all who reach out to Him in faith.
Pastor David W. Craig
Mount Pilgrim Baptist Church
Fairfield, Alabama

Dr. Hickman's faith has brought her through experiences that any other woman or even man would have given up on. In faith there is the seed of experience. Dr. Hickman shows in *All through Christ: Christ through All* that no matter what we face, God has given us the potential or capacity to develop into something great. We need God to teach us how to handle every situation.
Pastor Beverly M. Jackson
Church Of The Firstborn Ministries
Cottondale, Alabama

When you read, *All through Christ: Christ through All,* you will see that God is in the healing, restoring, and reconciling business. You will be encouraged that He proves His faithfulness and mercy through the hardest times of our lives. When I read Dr. Yvette Hickman's words, I hear the sound of grace that gives her strength and I see authentic faith that sustains her in her journey. I hope you will go on this journey with her. I know that your faith will be strengthened and your hope in the goodness of God will be renewed.
Pastor David Weir
Senior Pastor of Victory Church
Pell City, Alabama

Dr. Yvette Hickman, a Prophetic intercessor, Chaplain, and Poet has combined her many gifts to write a God inspired, bold, and revealing account of her many struggles as a Christian Physician. This account, a sequel to her book *Fountain in the Valley* demonstrates that God is faithful in our valley and mountain top experiences. A great Rx for encouragement for its readers.
Chaplain, Celia K. Boykins

Dr. Hickman is very thorough, concise, transparent, and gentle in her approach. With her relatable dialogue she makes the point no matter what you go through Christ is truly there in the midst of it all. She doesn't shy away from real-world issues and current topics plaguing our society all while tying in super-natural solutions. *All Through Christ: Christ through All* is very applicable to your life today. You will walk away from this book feeling that you have strengthened your spirit and be encouraged to dive deeper in your relationship with God.
Erika L. Mixon
Founder of Artrxbiz
Cover illustrator of *All through Christ: Christ through All*

# ALL THROUGH CHRIST: CHRIST THROUGH ALL

Dr. Yvette Hickman, MD

WESTBOW
PRESS®
A DIVISION OF THOMAS NELSON
& ZONDERVAN

WestBow Press books may be ordered through booksellers or by contacting:

WestBow Press
A Division of Thomas Nelson & Zondervan
1663 Liberty Drive
Bloomington, IN 47403
www.westbowpress.com
1 (866) 928-1240

Because of the dynamic nature of the Internet, any web addresses or links contained in
this book may have changed since publication and may no longer be valid. The views
expressed in this work are solely those of the author and do not necessarily reflect the views
of the publisher, and the publisher hereby disclaims any responsibility for them.

Any people depicted in stock imagery provided by Thinkstock are models,
and such images are being used for illustrative purposes only.
Certain stock imagery © Thinkstock.

ISBN: 978-1-5127-5706-4 (sc)
ISBN: 978-1-5127-5707-1 (hc)
ISBN: 978-1-5127-5705-7 (e)

Library of Congress Control Number: 2016915326

Print information available on the last page.

WestBow Press rev. date: 09/20/2016

# CONTENTS

# DEDICATION

This book is dedicated to my family. I thank the Lord for your understanding and patience as I fulfilled this assignment.

He is Alpha

# NO REGRETS

Living, Dying
Loving, Crying
Laughing, Wishing
NO REGRETS
No expiration dates stamped
NO MAN KNOWS
No matter what they proclaim
All, educated guesses
Predictions, estimations
All the same
The Truth is
NO MAN KNOWS
The hour or time
Our lives are given by
And, Returned to the
GIVER OF LIFE
YES
THE SPIRIT OF TRUTH
Proclaims
A child is born
YES
A Savior was given
YES
RISEN
We ALL have a time to be born
AND
A life to live

Each one with so much to give
A lineage to leave
A season to sow
A season to reap
A legacy to keep
Leave all you can
So the next generation
Can STAND
Speak Life
Pursue Peace
And Love ALL
This side of
Heaven's Walls

# FOREWORD

This is Dr. Yvette Hickman's second book and as the first it is penetrating and insightful. *All through Christ: Christ through All* is a holy blessing that will empower all Christians and direct those who are searching. This manuscript is not just for the up and up but also for the down and out. It encourages us to return back to the church as God's initial plan. *All through Christ: Christ through All* does not emphasize denomination but a live relationship with Jesus Christ.

Dr. Hickman is a great physician and in her medical profession she enables physical healing. She also encourages spiritual healing through a right relationship with God. She utilizes her spiritual gifts of wisdom and knowledge to promote both physical and spiritual healing for the glory of God. She is a prolific communicator who has a Christ centered medical calling. Her foundation as an author is the Bible. Her source of power is her Lord and Savior Jesus Christ.

Through insightful vision and articulation, *All through Christ: Christ through All*: emphasizes God's forgiveness when we did not deserve it; shows God's love as our power to serve; and encourages us in God's enabling power to do All through Christ that strengthens us. God is using Dr. Hickman to bring together a coalition of all ethnicities because God is concerned about every person. God is empowering us to be His supernatural and divine representatives in a world that has gone strongly astray. We need God's word to be our moral compass and His love. *All through Christ: Christ through All* encourages us to return back to God. In it Dr. Hickman also encourages communion with God and communication with each other. This phenomenal combination will take us as individuals as we read far beyond the tragedies of Minnesota, Louisiana and Dallas. You will be blessed as you read *All through Christ: Christ through All* as I was. Thank you Dr. Hickman for your spiritual words of wisdom and knowledge and helpful application for everyday living. I recommend this book with very high regards.

Dr. Barry Cosper

Bessemer Baptist Association Director of Missions

# INTRODUCTION

I have been a Board Certified Family Physician for nearly two decades. During my span of practice, I have been privileged to assist with the transition of life into this world and on to the next. In delivery rooms, I have had the blessing of being the first person to see a family's beautiful and new addition. I have also been honored to hold my patients' weakened and feeble hands as they took their final breath.

One truth remains the same through life's journey. Jesus is the Beginning and the End. He is Alpha and Omega. This is what *All Through Christ: Christ through All* is about. It is a journey through the good and bad times. It chronicles the last few years as seen through my eyes. Jesus is with us through it all. He was my New Beginning. He was the friend who stuck closer than a brother.

A palindrome is a word or group of words or numbers that reads the same backward or forward. The term is derived from the Greek term palin dromo which means running back again. The title of the book, *All through Christ: Christ through All* is a palindrome. This is significant because it symbolizes Christ's faithfulness. Jesus is the Beginning and the End. Christ was here when the world was framed. He still holds the earth together today. He is the same. God never changes.

I as many of you have quoted Philippians 4:13, "I can do all things through Christ who strengthens me." Often we quote this scripture when we are feeling strong and powerful. We proclaim it when things are going our way. But, Jesus is the way, truth and the life. Whether the way you are currently traveling is smooth or rocky, He is still the way. All through Christ in the good times such as during the birth of a child. Christ through all even at the death of a loved one. God is God in the valley low and on the mountain high. The prophet of old Isaiah exclaimed, "Every valley shall be exalted, and every mountain and hill shall be made low: and the crooked shall be made straight, and the rough places plain:"

Oftentimes we only need to look up and stop focusing on the problem. We just need to redirect our gaze to the problem solver. When we look to the hills which cometh our help then our vision and provision are no longer earth bound. Our Heavenly Father promises never to leave us nor forsake us. Jesus is our strength, our hope and our ever present help in our time of trouble. We can do all things through Him and He will be with us through it all. David beautifully recounted that he was once young but now he is old. He never saw the righteous forsaken nor his seed begging for bread. Scripture says that we overcome by the Blood of the Lamb. Jesus is that Lamb. He is the Lamb of God. God in His glorious love gave His only Son to die in our stead. The wages of sin is death but Glory to God, Jesus paid this price with His Blood. God is love and He showed His perfect love through Jesus. *All through Christ: Christ through All.*

We can do all through Christ. This is a testimony of His goodness and faithfulness. I have experienced His grace and mercy as I attained a medical degree without student loans. I recall praying prior to each test Philippians 4:13 and asking Holy Spirit to give me recollection of the material. I boast only on my God and not on my academic success. My faith was bolstered each time I quoted His Word. I recited that I could do all things through Christ until I believed that I could do all things through Christ that strengthens me.

I found myself as a Christian, black woman, in the predominately white male- dominated field of medicine. The focus was oftentimes placed on science rather than on faith. If you could not see something then it did not exist. I still walked by faith and not by sight. I learned to lean and rely on Christ through all. He did not let me fall. Early in my journey, on my first interview for medical school, the physician attempted to downplay my 3.95 undergraduate GPA. He made disparaging comments about HBCUs (Historically Black Colleges and Universities). The doctor who would one day be my colleague thumbed through my application and callously said, "We all know that black colleges overinflate their GPAs". I would like to encourage the readers that no weapon formed against you shall prosper. What God has for you, it is for you. I repeat that I am now his colleague. I am his peer. There is no fear in Christ.

Interestingly while I was working on this portion of the book, the now deceased Supreme Court Justice Antonin Scalia made equally appalling comments. During his oral argument regarding affirmative action he referred to some colleges as less-advanced. He referred to certain universities as slower track schools. These comments were made decades later by two distinct individuals. In my opinion they shared the same heart. Scripture says that the issues of life flow from the heart.

Within the same week Presidential Candidate Donald Trump added the following initiative to his platform's discriminatory rhetoric. He suggested banning the entrance of Muslims to the United States. Supreme Court Justice Scalia, Donald Trump and my colleague's comments contained the same message of bigotry. President Obama cautioned Americans in a speech that commemorated the 150th anniversary of the 13th Amendment. As we recall the 13th Amendment abolished slavery. The first African-American President said, "We betray the efforts of the past if we fail to push back against bigotry in all its forms." The emphasis of *All through Christ: Christ through All* is our victory in Christ. Do not allow yourself to become a victim of another's perception of you. We can do all through Christ because He lives within us. He reigns so we reign.

The events around the world during the development of this book were tumultuous. I was led to begin an international internet based call in radio show, What up Doc?. Many of the topics for chapters in this book were inspired by feedback from the callers. Glory to God, Christ is still King of kings as we navigate the new world order.

I recall as a young doctor in training examining a belligerent patient, who attempted to kick me and called me a racial slur. I was trying to listen to her heart and breath sounds. Another incident is seared into my consciousness but praise God not engraved in my heart. An elderly woman proclaimed on her death bed that she would rather die than let a Black take care of her. Some things are matters of the heart. Decades may change but hearts may stay the same. Holy Spirit convicts and pricks but it is still our choice whether to change.

I was told that my previous book, *Fountain in the Valley* was a how-to- manual on GETTING out of the valley of life. I pray that *All through Christ: Christ through All* will be a how-to-manual on STAYING out of the valley. People graciously allowed me to share their testimonies of God's healing power and deliverance. I candidly stated in the introduction of *Fountain in the Valley* that I was in a valley during most of the writing of that book. I did not divulge what or who was attempting to keep me in the valley. *All through Christ: Christ through All* includes my personal testimony of God's faithfulness and mercy in my life. Racism, hatred and bigotry are valleys that try to hold the souls of God's people captive. But, God is our sustainer and our deliverer. Isaiah 41:17-18 reads, "When the poor and needy seek water, and there is none, and their tongue faileth for thirst, I the Lord will hear them, I the God of Israel will not forsake them. I will open rivers in high places, and fountains in the midst of the valleys: I will make the wilderness a pool of water and the dry land springs of water."

God is love and scripture describes Him as the Father of Lights. In God there is not even the shadow of turning. His light shines a light on areas of personal and systemic darkness. Light always dispels darkness. Darkness can no longer exist where light is present. Jesus is the light of the world and His light prevails. Through it all, which includes the good and the bad, we can do all through Christ. Christ is Our Light in darkness.

I was sharing a rhema word with a sister in Christ. I heard the words, "as easy as 1, 2, 3". I saw in the spirit, a beautiful water fall and a home with red accents in the spirit. A rhema word is colloquially known as a "right now" word. It is an utterance inspired by Holy Spirit that deals with a specific situation. In contrast, logos is the written, infallible Word of God. We were praying regarding her job situation. After that rhema word was released she was offered an administrative position at an elementary school. She had previously been out of work and essentially homeless. True to the prophetic word her new job had a water fall in the lobby. Within two months she closed on a lovely brick home with red shutters. To God be the glory for the things He has done. When I shared the rhema words that I received with that faith-filled woman of God her response was consistent. She would say "I believe God". The word, "as easy as 1, 2, 3", indicated her new job educating our youth in their "A, B, C's and 1, 2, 3's". It also spoke to my spirit as well. I was led to research the prophetic meanings of numbers. Each chapter number has spiritual significance in this book.

We are directed by God to walk by faith and not by sight. I pray that you are blessed by my walk of faith as I share my journey in *All Through Christ: Christ through All.*

# CHAPTER 1

# UNITY THROUGH CHRIST

# UNITY THROUGH CHRIST

**I Timothy 2:5** *For there is one God, and one mediator between God and men, the man Christ Jesus;*

Jesus is the beginning and the end. He is Alpha and Omega. Jesus is the one who was and is to come. He is the only begotten Son of God. In Him all things were created and in Him we move and have our being. Jesus existed before all and He holds all creation together. Our God is Ancient of Days. Jesus is the WAY, the truth and the life. That begs the question. Which WAY are you choosing to go? One of my favorite quotes is by my previous pastor, Bishop Jim Lowe. He often says, "Life is choice driven and you live and you die by the choices you make." We are faced, moment by moment, with seemingly insignificant decisions. These choices in actuality can not only impact us but also may affect many others including generations to come.

No man is an island. No matter how independent and self-sufficient we want or claim to be we are interrelated and interdependent on each other. We do have different strengths but we ultimately need and rely on our fellow man. Another person's decisions affect us positively or negatively and vice versa. We have all heard the saying that your rights stop where another person's begins. There is a cautionary tale about freedom of speech. Our rights do not include maliciously yelling, "FIRE" in a crowded public place.

Three brothers from Melbourne Australia took social media by storm. Many are calling their videos insensitive and insidious. The trio dressed in traditional Arabian clothing threw black duffle bags in a public places. They then suddenly ran away insinuating the contents were bombs.

The clips have received millions of views. The victims of the pranks responses were the same until the trio's fourth video. The surprised and horrified people would usually run in fear screaming. One man even jumped into a lake to escape the infamous black bag. The not-so-funny joke turned on the "Jalals" as they refer to themselves. They received an unexpected reaction during the taping of their final video. One of the brothers was shot in the abdomen by his terrified target.

We have rights but our rights end when they encroach upon others' safety. Political candidates who, from their platform, make cruel and untrue generalizations, in my opinion, are eliciting riots. People were punched by candidates' supporters at political rallies. A Muslim woman was escorted out while people hurled insults at her. She was simply standing in silent protest. Riots have erupted thus far in Chicago and New Mexico during this political vetting process. The line of freedom of speech and starting a riot has been blurred in "my country tis of thee, sweet land of liberty". There have been many inciting rather than insightful remarks made by hate mongers. I believe their goal is to divide, "one nation under God, indivisible …". I once heard a preacher say that God specializes in addition and multiplication not subtraction and division. Jesus multiplied the fish and loaves of bread from a young lad's lunch and fed the multitude. God commanded Adam and Eve in the Garden of Eden to be fruitful and multiply. Multiplication and not division is God's preferred mathematical operation.

In a city near where I work, worship and raise my family, divisive literature has been appearing in yards and on car windshields. The local branch of a white supremacist group distributed flyers near my neighborhood. Many people in 2016 woke up to recruiting literature on their property picturing a man robed in a white sheet pointing and saying, "The KKK Wants You!" We as a country need to wake up. We hear the chant, "Make America Great Again" on the evening news. How about, "Make America in God We Trust Again and One Nation Under God Again". God is love and He is a God of multiplication and not division.

The flyer's recruiting rhetoric continued by urging people to join the fight of the "spread of Islam in our country". These propagandist ploys played out on the heels of the internationally heart-wrenching mass shooting in Paris. Days later a national unnatural disaster hit California. Fourteen people were murdered and twenty-two injured by "radicalized extremist" while attending an office Christmas party. There is a problem in the world but we need to build bridges rather than build walls. Isolation and division only breed contempt and more misunderstanding. Only love conquers hate. Hatred self-propagates. It spreads like a cancer until all involved are destroyed.

Dr. Martin Luther King wrote *A Letter from a Birmingham Jail* more than 50 years ago but truth stands forever. He wrote, "Moreover, I am cognizant of the interrelatedness of all communities and states. I cannot sit idly by in Atlanta and not be concerned about what happens in Birmingham. Injustice anywhere is a threat to justice everywhere. We are caught in an inescapable network of mutuality, tied in a single garment of destiny. Whatever affects one directly, affects all indirectly." The media reports that these modern day tragedies were propagated by "radicalized" Muslim terrorists. The working definition of the term "radicalized" seems to only apply to believers in Islam. A radical is an individual who has adopted extreme views or patterns of belief outside of the parameters of the norm regarding social, political or religious ideals. The Ku Klux Klan reports that they are a Christian organization. One of their main agendas is to promote Christian values. This begs the question are they then radicalized Christian terrorists?

One of my mentors shared a powerful testimony of God's love with me. It has changed my life and world view. Dr. Cosper was preaching the Word of God to a racially diverse group of believers. He was prompted by the Holy Spirit to encourage the Christians in attendance to find someone they did not know and if possible someone who did not look like them. He asked them to pray with and for them. I can't emphasize this theme enough in *All Through Christ: Christ through All*. God is a God of love .That being said I propose that prayer is our love language. Prayer transcends our human weaknesses and biases. Praying for your enemies allows God's power to work in your heart as well as in others' lives. Prayer is not just a mental exercise of recitation and repetition. The issues of your heart are released and entrusted to a willing and able God. James Goll writes in his book on intercessory prayer, "Not only does the Holy Spirit have a deep love language that He will express through us, but He will arise at times with the righteous indignation of God and wage war through His people. This is the intercessory and spiritual warfare posture. Obstacles stand in the way of God's purposes, but the Holy Spirit will step up to the plate and pronounce the will of God through His yielded vessels, using a language that goes beyond natural words."

The prayers of the righteous do avail much. Dr. Cosper saw from a bird's eye view a mighty work of God as he ministered from the pulpit at this prayer meeting in the Deep South. As a yielded vessel of God and prayer warrior he witnessed the power of prayer. Self -proclaimed members of the KKK prayed with and tearfully embraced fellow members of the Body of Christ that happened to be African American. As the tears flowed the shackles of racism also fell. People united under God wept with their brothers in Christ. They realized they were children of the same God. Some just happened to have more melanin in their skin than others. Dr. Martin Luther King eloquently said, "Darkness cannot drive out darkness: only light can do that. Hate cannot drive out hate: only love can do that."

I was blessed to work with Dr. Cosper and a local hospital chaplain to institute and proliferate a multidenominational and multiethnic community prayer breakfast. The Spirit of Truth, which is God's Holy

Spirit met with us month after month. Many pastors and political leaders beseeched God's will on earth as it is in heaven. Dennis Fuqua in his book on corporate prayer says, "On many occasions I have had my understanding of Jesus Christ enlarged and even corrected as I have heard the prayers of people who know Christ differently than I have known him." I was given the privilege to address the group with a few brief words of encouragement. I then humbly led these men and women in prayer. Many had been in the ministry longer than I have been alive. This gathering included one illustrious mayor who is the son and grandson of preachers.

I began the discussion with the pots that I saw in the vision that inspired *Fountain in the Valley.* I explained that the pots actually represented earthen vessels or us as believers. The pots were initially so dirty and filled with so much hatred, bitterness and bigotry that you could not see the beautiful calling for their lives. Hidden under the pot's filth was engraved a scripture out of Zechariah. The inscription read "Holiness Unto the Lord". Glory to God by the washing of our Savior's Blood and the purging by the fire of Truth the beautiful calling was revealed. Under the grime and grit we are God's chosen vessels. We are His royal priesthood. And whether we are black, white, young, old, male, female, rich or poor, we make up the Body of Christ.

We then all prayed from pastors to politicians for God's will to be done on earth as it is in heaven. This beautiful scene was imprinted on my heart. I looked out at the crowd and saw big, small, old, young, dark and light hands clasped together in prayer. I saw unity in Christ. We are the hands and feet of Jesus. An image of eternity emerged in my spirit man. As we prayed, I saw God's will on earth as it is in heaven. We are united under God.

I was blessed to attend a majority Caucasian church during last Christmas season. My heart was pricked as we sang, "O Holy Night". We sing this classic holiday hymn at my predominately African-American home church as well. The words in verse three resonated in and renewed my mind this particular Sunday. The congregation sang, "Truly He taught us to love one another; His law is love and His gospel is peace. Chains shall He break, for the slave is our brother, And in His name all oppression shall cease." God is love and we demonstrate that love by being our brother's keeper and not our brother's oppressor.

God is love. Christians and Muslims have certain basic core beliefs. Members of the Body of Christ who have wandered out of the boundary of love have wandered from the core belief of Christianity. God is love and love does not promote or propagate hate and fear. Scripture reminds us that perfect love casts out fear. True love does not foster and cultivate fear. A tree is known by its fruit. If you proclaim to be a follower of a loving God then your fruit will be love and not fear or hate. One of my favorite scriptures is contained in I Corinthians where Paul eloquently defines love as kind and not easily provoked. Apostle Paul continues expressing the eternal fact that love does not rejoice in iniquity but rejoices in the truth.

While I was in prayer the days prior to the San Bernardino shooting, I heard the words, "spirit of truth". I was led to pray regarding God's Spirit of Truth resting, ruling and abiding in our world. The prayer burden was so heavy that I elicited assistance from other intercessors. James Goll explains in his book on intercessor prayer, "As it is in the natural, so it is in the spiritual. Travail is a form of intense intercession given by the Holy Spirit whereby an individual or group is gripped by a gestating promise that grips God's heart. The individual or group labors with Him in prayer so that the new life can come forth." I am part of the intercessory prayer ministry at my local church. We are well versed in "praying the scriptures". We are trained to make our unique and specific petitions known to our loving and faithful God by praying His Word back to Him. Isaiah 43:26 confirms this practice. It reads, "Put me in remembrance: let us plead together: declare thou, that thou mayest be justified."

Prior to the shooting, I was led to base my prayers from John 16:13, NIV. "But when he, the Spirit of truth, comes, he will guide you into all the truth. He will not speak on his own; he will speak only what he hears, and he will tell you what is yet to come." I asked for the Spirit of Truth to dispel the darkness and for divine revelation. There was still a burning in my spirit. There was an unction to continue interceding even though I did not know about what or for whom. I only knew there was unrest in the spiritual realm and Holy Spirit was urging me to intercede. Romans 8:26 explains, "Likewise the Spirit also helpeth our infirmities: for we know not what we should pray for as we ought: but the Spirit itself maketh intercession for us with groanings which cannot be uttered."

I was later directed to read and meditate upon 1 John 4:3-6. These scriptures provided understanding and helped relieve my prayer burden. It reads, "And every spirit that confesseth not that Jesus Christ is come in the flesh is not of God: and this is that Spirit of antichrist, whereof ye have heard that it should come; and even now already is it in the world. Ye are of God, little children, and have overcome them: because greater is He that is in you, than he that is in the world. They are of the world: therefore speak they of the world, and the world heareth them. We are of God: he that knoweth God heareth us; he that is not of God heareth not us. Hereby know we the spirit of truth, and the spirit of error." The Kingdom of God is greater than the kingdom of darkness. Light will prevail. The victory has already been won through Christ. We have a role to play but let not our hearts be troubled. Jesus has overcome the world and we overcome the enemy by His Blood. The battle was won by Jesus's redemptive work on the cross. He is the light of the world and we are of Him. Even though things look dark we are to still let our light shine. A glimmer of light creates enough love to dispel darkness. Don't lose heart. Don't lose hope. Don't be ashamed of the gospel of Jesus Christ. Display your light which radiates from the Father of Light. Magnify and reflect His love so that all the earth can see Him through you. I Corinthians 13:12 reads, "For now we see through a glass, darkly; but then face to face: now I know in part; but then shall I know even as also I am known."

Over the last three months during my morning time of prayer and meditation I have been led to study the books of Isaiah and Revelation. Revelation is the testimony of the Lord Jesus Christ. He is the Beginning and the End. He is Alpha and Omega. Jesus is the Word of God made flesh. Isaiah 8:22 reads, "And they shall look to the earth; and behold trouble and darkness, dimness of anguish; and they shall be driven to darkness." God is not mocked and what He says is the Truth. Knowledge is power but true wisdom only comes from God. God is All Powerful and All Knowing. He is omnipotent and omniscient. I strive to put you in remembrance that our God is love and the Greater One does live in us. God is merciful and slow to wrath. His warning does come before destruction. We should try to obtain unity through Christ because united we stand. Divided we fall.

My professor in the School of the Prophets is Prophet Joe Brock. He cautioned us a year or so ago that we are not to be puffed up because we can predict a tragedy. We should instead intercede that our predictions of darkness do not come true. As prophetic intercessors we should see in the spirit the plans of the enemy but our ultimate goal is to never see them in the natural. Intercession halts the hand of the enemy and thwarts his evil schemes. Prophet Brock instructed us regarding experiencing visions and dreams from the second heaven. They give us a glance into the enemy's war room. This allows God's people the ability to strategize intercessory and natural counter attacks. The weapons of our warfare are not carnal. We are spirit beings living in physical bodies. We are fighting a spiritual warfare. We cannot be tempted to fight in the flesh a battle that can only be won by spiritual means. Don't get me wrong. I don't sit around all day praying. I seek God's direction and get my marching orders. I then do what the Lord commands me to do in the earth realm.

Prophet Brock prophesied of black water and the smell of death at a conference in Louisiana months prior to the BP oil spill. This national disaster devastated the United States in 2010. Scripture says that warning comes before destruction. The Sovereign LORD does nothing without revealing His plan to his servants, the prophets. Prophet Brock urged congregations everywhere he ministered to pray against this ominous vision. The damage was horrendous but much more damage and loss of life was probably aborted. The prayers of the righteous sparked by Prophet Brock's call to intercession availed much. James Goll in his book, *The Prophetic Intercessor* writes, "There are many lessons to grasp here- but let's keep it simple. God speaks. Man hears. Faith is sparked. Man responds to the spark of faith and prays the promise into being. Tenacity and endurance are required when the desired result seems to be delayed. Even when the breakthrough begins, it takes eyes of discernment to recognize it."

It is still unusual and uncommon to hear a prophet say that they would rather their predictions not come to pass. They are then truly seeking the greater good for man and the will of God. James Goll explains, "Prophecy, we could say, is the expressed thought of God delivered in a manner that no person in his or her natural talent or knowledge could ever fully articulate. The substance and nature of prophecy is supernatural, coming from the heart of God into the heart and mind of a person by the gifts of the Holy Spirit." God is love and His servant's should show His love by not being puffed up and vaunting themselves. Love is patient and love is kind. It does not envy and it does not boast. Love is not proud nor is God's servants. God is love and we should show His love through our service and unity. *All through Christ: Christ through All.*

**I Timothy 2:5** *For there is one God, and one mediator between God and men, the man Christ Jesus;*

# NOTES

# CHAPTER 2

# TESTIMONY THROUGH CHRIST

# TESTIMONY THROUGH CHRIST

**Mark 6:7** *And he called unto him the twelve, and began to send them forth by two and two; and gave them power over unclean spirits;*

The number two symbolizes a witness. A witness attests that what another is saying is an accurate account. The Bible says that matters should be confirmed by the testimony of two or more witnesses. Two can also symbolize unity, strength and companionship. James Goll in his guide on defeating demonic strongholds and oppression explains, "A testimony is given by a witness. The word for witness in Greek is martus, from which we get our English word martyr. The word implies that one who will testify to Jesus' sacrifice on the cross would be willing to speak about it even if that costs him his life."

The animals entered the ark two by two and Jesus sent His disciples out in twos. There is strength in numbers. One main tactic of the enemy is to isolate so that he can divide and conquer. God proclaimed in Genesis that it is not good for man to be alone. So, He gave Eve to Adam as a help mate. The book of Ecclesiastes explains in simple terms that if a person is walking alone and falls he has no one to help him up. We all fall down. Proverbs says that a righteous man falls down seven times but he gets back up. I might fall down but don't count me out. I serve a forgiving and merciful God. We all make mistakes. We all have sinned and fall short of the glory of God. God is faithful to forgive if we humble ourselves and ask for forgiveness. He is faithful to help us if we humble ourselves and ask for His help.

We are our brother's keeper. Praise God that He is our Keeper. One of the most beautiful bonds that I have been privileged to witness is that of one man and one woman united in holy matrimony. I have cared for people in my medical practice until truly death did them part. I have been privileged to see elderly couples married 40, 50, 60 plus years caring and taking care of each other. They push one another in wheelchairs. They provide each other meals in bed when their spouse becomes too ill to come to the dinner table. This is truly in sickness and in health. It warms my heart to see God's love in action. I've seen respect and love grow even as sexual ability, mental capacity and physical endurance diminish.

One such couple was only married a few years before their vows were tested. I have witnessed their wonderful testimony of love despite a devastating medical disability. The young couples' plans were drastically altered when the vibrant and jovial wife experienced a ruptured brain aneurysm. Her quick wit and hilarious humor was slowed. She now struggles to find her next word in just a day to day conversation. Her motor skills were drastically affected. The once diva can no longer apply her makeup or comb her own hair. Despite her limitations her hair and makeup have been perfectly styled on each visit. Her burly, husband coifs her hair, applies her eyeshadow, lipstick and blush daily. He lovingly extends her contracted fingers and treats his bride to a weekly manicure.

This testimony of a husband loving his wife as Christ loves the church blesses my soul. He put his career on hold to become his wife's caregiver. Love is what love does. I have never sensed any resentment or bitterness from him. This young husband only shows acceptance and love to his disabled wife. He listens intently and patiently as she tells her jokes. They are still ever so funny but it takes her a little longer to tell them. I have been blessed to learn so much about the Fruit of the Spirit from this couple. Love is kind, patient, and longsuffering. Love never fails.

In contrast I have seen a trend over the last decade of college educated, self-sufficient women who sacrifice their marriages for their careers. Their motto has become, "I can bring home the bacon and fry it up in a pan so I really don't have need for a man." I have witnessed wives publically emasculate their husbands. They systematically neuter them insult by insult as disparaging word after disparaging word is hurled. The assailant later complains that their husband will not stand up and be the man. James warns that the tongue is small yet powerful. It is able to set the course of nature on fire with its deadly poison. We, as women are naturally nurturers. We were created to be a help-mate not to create a stalemate. Proverbs 14:1 NLT reads, "A wise woman builds her home, but a foolish woman tears it down with her own hands."

When I married more than 20 years ago, my grandmother told me, "It is good to have a man around the house". My then 70 year old grandmother advised me to cook for my husband. She would say with a smile, "and not just in the kitchen." As a physician my salary often has nearly doubled my spouses. Regardless, I respect him as the head of our household. This lesson was not one that I learned easily. Hopefully you can learn vicariously through my mistakes and testimony. I initially had misgivings about why certain luxuries that I wanted did not fit in the family budget. As I matured I learned the difference between a need and a want. I learned to compromise.

I had serious trust issues when I married at 21 years old. My parents' as well as my paternal grandparents' marriages ended in divorce. My matriarchs struggled financially to raise their children. I kept this painful past in the back of my mind. Early in my marriage I had an exit plan that would allow me to travel lightly and quickly. I now regret limiting the number of off springs our union produced because of the fear of abandonment. I selfishly contemplated the potential end of my marriage more than the beginning of another life. I was haunted by the failed marriages of my ancestors. I allowed their past pain and regrets to limit my future happiness. I subconsciously pushed my husband away with hurtful words and inconsiderate actions. I was afraid to love. Paul wrote of man's irrational and sometimes schizophrenic behavior in Roman 7:15, "For that which I do I allow not: for what I would, that do I not; but what I hate, that do I."

I had said, "I do", but was looking for a reason to say I don't. I wanted an out clause. My un-renewed mind sought a reason to leave him before he left me. I was caught up in a pattern of self-fulfilling prophecy. Paul in the book of Romans verse 12:2 admonishes us to, "And be not conformed to this world: but be ye transformed by the renewing of your mind, that ye may prove what is that good, and acceptable, and perfect, will of God." I unknowingly allowed the thing I feared most for my young marriage to stalk me. The acronym F.E.A.R. stands for false experiences appearing real. I knew that I was exhibiting self-destructive behaviors that were counterproductive to a healthy and thriving relationship. Knowing is only half the battle. I had to be willing to make the necessary steps to change.

On one hand I wanted the wall around my heart. It shielded and protected me from my fear of abandonment. On the other hand I deeply desired my husband's love and intimacy. Prayer, godly counsel and an humbling separation allowed me to accept my spouse's love. I learned through a near break-up and a broken heart to accept my husband. I received his affection rather than always trying to analyze or control it. I have read and recommended many books to patients over the years. This one in particular assisted me in seeing my shortcomings. Stormie Omartian in her book, *The Power of a Praying Wife* writes, " …relying on God's power to transform you, your husband, your circumstances, and your marriage. This power is not given to wield like a weapon in order to beat back an unruly beast. It's a gentle tool of restoration appropriated through the prayers of a wife who longs to do right more than be right, and to give life more than get even." I needed prayer and God's power to heal my broken heart. My brokenness stemmed from betrayals that occurred years before even meeting my husband. I like many of you brought baggage filled with trash from my past into my present. I allowed the garbage I brought with me to stink up my present. God allowed me to see my shortcomings and stop blaming my discontentment on my husband. Matthew 7:5 reads, "Thou hypocrite, first cast out the beam out of thine own eye; and then shalt thou see clearly to cast out the mote out of thy brother's eye."

I was harboring unforgiveness and resentment in my heart. I had a deep void in my soul. I was unfairly looking to a mere man to fill a hole only God could fill. We should look to God to make us whole and not people or things. I needed the lover of my soul to heal and to deliver me. As I committed myself and my past mistakes to God, I saw myself and others through God's grace. I was able to forgive myself and others. I attempted to bridge the fractured relationship with my biological father before his untimely death. I placed the poem that begins this book, "No Regrets" on the printed program for his funeral. I eventually learned how to let my husband off the hook for my happiness. I sought God's peace and this translated to true joy. God restored unto me the joy of my salvation. Stormie Omartian says, " …often a couple will have preconceived ideas about who the other is and how married life is supposed to be, and then reality hits. That's when their kingdom can become divided. You have to continually pray that any unreal expectations be exposed and all incompatibilities be smoothed out so that you grow together in a spirit of unity, commitment, and a bond of intimacy."

Marriage is a holy union that is ordained by God. Scripture lovingly describes believers as the Bride of Christ. Husbands are directed in Ephesians to love their wives as Christ loved the Church. I was volunteering at a young women's conference. One of the professors lovingly shared spiritual truths on misaligned love. The audience was 15-21 year old females. I was previously unfamiliar with the term misaligned love. Her talk imparted wisdom to not just the young women in the room but to me as well. This concept of misaligned love put many things into perspective for us. The instructor explained how the enemy is a deceiver and a counterfeiter. One of his tactics is misconstruing and misaligning what was initially meant as good or holy. The enemy was once the praise and worship leader in heaven. But, because of jealousy he attempted to usurp God's authority. The devil desired to steal God's worship and adoration. Satan convinced one third of the angels to misalign their love and loyalty .He convinced them to serve him rather than the One, True God. The enemy had the audacity to spark a revolt against the maker of heaven and earth. The devil was the one seen falling from heaven as lightening, despite his deception. The truth always prevails and God always wins. Revelation 12:9 reads, "And the great dragon was cast out, that old serpent, called the Devil, and Satan, which deceiveth the whole world: he was cast out into the earth, and his angels were cast out with him." That was our first example of the consequences of MISALIGNED LOVE. Any love that does not line up with the Word of God is misaligned love.

Most of the young ladies were high school and college students. The teacher warned them about potentially abusive and controlling relationships. She cautioned that a suitor can initially present himself as kind and caring. This fake persona will eventually fade. It then reveals their true color as green. Jealous behavior is not a sign of love but of MISALIGNED LOVE. Many women have heard after a savage beating at the hands of their boyfriends or husbands this saying. The men claim that they only did it because they loved them. The abuser often continues that the beating was for their own good and it was the woman's fault. A few years ago, after the video of the NFL player dragging his unconscious girlfriend surfaced, I hosted a domestic violence symposium. I was led to gather survivors of domestic violence, advocate agencies, female physicians and lawyers. We focused our teen-aged girls conference topics on peer pressure, bullying and domestic violence. The accustomation to such brutal and demeaning treatment is a systematic process. Our goal was to build self-esteem and teach the warning signs of domestic abuse. I am a firm believer that it does take a village to raise a child.

The world witnessed through the media's coverage and social media what an elevator's surveillance camera captured. I believe we saw publically what had been occurring privately. The couple had been together since high school. In my experience such savage abuse does not start overnight. Scripture says that warning comes before destruction. Often there are warning signs early. Curt words and snide remarks often progress to physical violence. Our initiative was to present warning signs to the youth. We offered them skills through role play and lectures to recognize and potentially escape this spiral of demise.

A person can have the "birth position" of a mother, father, sister or brother. If that bond is not nurtured it is in name only. Don't be a Christian or a parent in name only. Actions speak louder than words. Faith without works is dead. Talk without the walk is living a lie. Without the love of Christ our homes and vows dwindle. This leads to broken hearts and promises. We have to be Born Again or accept Jesus as Our Personal Savior in order to mend our broken relationship with God. Christ paid the debt that our sin caused. Jesus is our propitiation for our sins. He paid the cost for our salvation with His Blood on the cross. Jesus is the Savior of the world. He is the King of kings and Lord of lords. It is still our choice to crown Him Lord of our lives. God gives us freewill to accept or reject His Only Begotten Son. God desires submitted and obedient servants. The enemy in contrast desires to coerce, control and enslave us to a life of sin.

My pastor, Dr. David Craig preached a series of sermons on the difference between the terms relationship and position. God is not impressed by our positions, titles or degrees. He is instead looking for a personal and intimate relationship with us through His Son. He is looking for people with contrite hearts who are willing and available. Position is a direct result of godly relationship. We should seek first the kingdom of God then He promises to provide our needs. God gives the increase to people He can trust with His treasures. Relationship is also a direct result of position. Pastor Craig described people sitting at varying distances around a camp fire. He said, "You have to be in close proximity to feel the heat and you should seek to follow God closer to know Him better." Scripture encourages us that if we draw near to God that He will draw near to us. God is beckoning us to come in closer to Him. Seek a closer relationship with the true lover of our souls. Isaiah 66:2 reads, "For all those things hath mine hand made, and all those things have been, saith the LORD: but to this man will I look, even to him that is poor and of a contrite spirit, and trembleth at my word."

As a physician, part of my job is to instruct people on healthy living. When I am graced to see patients overcome their various ills it inspires me. One such encounter occurred recently. I was blessed to meet a survivor of a horrific closed head injury. She still suffered from a seizure disorder resulting from the trauma. Over my years in the ministry and in medicine I have learned never to look disparagingly upon anyone. You know where you have been but you do not know where you are going. I am retelling her story to potentially save someone's life and not to condemn hers. Paul reminds the Church of Corinth in I Corinthians 6:11, "And such were some of you: but ye are washed, but ye are sanctified, but ye are justified in the name of the Lord Jesus, and by the Spirit of our God." Everyone has a past. Some of us were able to make it out of ours without bumps and bruises. Other people were not.

I was impressed and intrigued by this woman's positive outlook and upbeat conversation. She spoke about the goodness of God despite having obvious facial deformity and speech abnormality. This woman is a living testimony of God's grace. She is also a survivor of misaligned love. Her misaligned love was in the form of domestic abuse. She told me how her "old man" turned violent one night. She reported that he attacked her after her shift in the parking lot of her job. The woman's "lover" hit her over the head with a metal car jack. He then pushed her lifeless body into the trunk of her own car. He drove her to a secluded location where he beat and raped her. She lives to warn others of the vicious cycle of abuse. She is now wiser and stronger. The woman once naively bragged to her friends before the murder attempt that "he is so cute when he is jealous". A person shows you who they are. But it is our responsibility to believe them when they show us. Warning comes before destruction. This woman is alive despite physical and emotional scars. Many others of domestic abuse are not. This is a wake -up call for someone. I urge you to take heed to the warning.

She escaped with her life and praise God with her peace of mind. She was able to forgive her assailant. Forgiveness does not mean she did not press charges. She did seek justice and "the love of her life" is still in prison. This strong woman is a survivor. She did not allow misaligned love to continue to steal from her. She forgave. She did not allow unforgiveness and bitterness to rob her of her joy and peace. The joy of the Lord is our strength but the enemy comes to steal, kill and destroy. I praise God that Jesus came so that we might have life more abundantly. God is true love. He is not a misaligned love.

I had the opportunity to discuss many hot news topics on my radio call in show, What up Doc? One episode focus was on the arrest of county clerk Kim Davis. This brave woman refused to grant a marriage certificate to a same sex couple in Kentucky. She was jailed for five days for contempt of court. Mrs. Davis is a Christian and issuing marriage licenses to gay couples was against her moral conscious. The courageous county clerk stood on the Biblical definition of marriage. God's law supports one man and one woman being joined in holy matrimony. Much misaligned love starts on a slippery slope. Some people argue that love is love and they can't choose who they fall in love with. We all are tempted with sensual and fleshly desires. It is our choice to corral our ungodly desires into the constraints of the Word of God. Our temptations are not always the same but we all have temptations. Yours might be different than mine but we all have temptations. Yours might be a beautiful girl while mine could be a handsome man. The truth is that any sexual activity not in the confines of God's definition of holy matrimony is wrong. Wrong is wrong no matter how many laws say it is right.

I make no difference between or excuses for heterosexual sins of fornication and adultery or homosexual sin. Scripture says that the wages of sin is death. HIV does not discriminate between gay, straight, male, female, black, white, young, old, rich or poor. Current statistics in the United States show that our future leaders aged 20-24 have the highest rates of new HIV infections. No matter what the commercials may say condoms make sex safer and not safe. I treat STD's on a weekly basis in my medical practice. Many were contracted despite the use of condoms. The media promotes promiscuity. It does not give equal air time to the devastating and sometimes deadly consequences of such dangerous choices.

I was appalled by the former madam, Heidi Fleiss. She made media attention after releasing her high profile client list. A reporter asked her if her "girls" used condoms with Charlie Sheen. He was one of Heidi's regulars who has since admitted to having HIV. Heidi answered that whether or not to wear condoms was the worker's choice and the client's preference. She candidly admitted that many of her sex workers do not insist on condoms during paid sexual services. The millionaire madam went on to flippantly say, on primetime TV that HIV is "like asthma, big deal, so you take some medication. It's NOT a death sentence or something." This permissive attitude is pervasive in our country. The truth is that over a million people worldwide have died every year of AIDS related causes over the last decade. Ephesians 2:2-4 reads, "Wherein in time past ye walked according to the course of this world, according to the prince of the power of the air, the spirit that now worketh in the children of disobedience: Among whom also we all had our conversation in times past in the lusts of our flesh, fulfilling the desires of the flesh and of the mind; and were by nature the children of wrath, even as others. But God, who is rich in mercy, for his great love wherewith he loved us," God's love is true and pure. It is not misguided or misaligned.

Misaligned love is misaligned love. It does not matter whether it is in a gay or straight relationship. As a family physician I have seen in the last few years more teenagers and young adults in gender identity crisis than in prior years of practice. The media is pushing misalignment of love. TV shows are promoting a "new norm". Same sex couples blatantly display intimacy during prime time programming. This was once considered family viewing time. This is in an attempt to infiltrate the minds of our children. The prince of the power of the air is utilizing the airwaves to push, promote and peddle his wicked agenda. A well-known male Olympian was on the Wheaties's box when I was a child. He has now transitioned to a woman. She has now posed on the cover of Vanity Fair with a swimsuit on.

Children saw images of a father and grandfather on a primetime television program. The popular programming displays the lifestyle of this celebrity family. On the next season's episodes our nation's confused youth saw the show's Paw-Paw wearing a dress. She now has HER own T.V. show. She asks the world to call her by her new female name. Ephesians 6:12 explains that, "For we wrestle not against flesh and blood, but against principalities, against powers, against the rulers of the darkness of this world, against spiritual wickedness in high places." James Goll explains in *Deliverance from Darkness* that, "The phrase spiritual wickedness in high places paints a picture of hosts of evil in the unseen realm—countless foot soldiers that are under the control of satan, has fallen angelic princes and his world dominators. These foot-soldier demons are lower spirits that have established strongholds in individuals, families, neighborhoods and cities."

Cindy Trimm in her book on spiritual warfare says, "The next question is, what rules the earth? As long as man does not take his rightful stance, posture, and place in God through prayer, evil and evil human beings will rule. Herein lies the challenge. You must arise and take your place so that through you God can restore order, peace, righteousness, morality, ethics, just governance, health, and healing." I have had the opportunity to hear Dr. Trimm speak on several occasions. One engagement specifically stands out in my mind. She was speaking at a church in Birmingham. While in the pulpit introducing her topic she said, "I have my message prepared but God wants this to be a deliverance service." She spent the next hour praying for the multitudes gathered in the name of the Lord Jesus. I was amazed then and still am awe struck at God's power demonstrated that Saturday afternoon. Dr. Trimm began walking from the front of the sanctuary to the back. As she prayed and laid hands on the person on the end of each row that person and the others on that row fell like dominoes. Many were slain in the Holy Spirit. Displays of God's deliverance continued row by row and section by section. Matthew 12:28 explains, "But if I cast out devils by the Spirit of God, then the kingdom of God is come unto you." Prayer works. God is still a deliverer but He does not overrule our free will. Freedom is available through Christ but the choice is ours.

I take care of respectfully and proficiently many same sex couples and gay individuals in my medical practice. I offer advice and guidance for them to lead healthy and happy lives. I don't force my beliefs on another person. I foster an environment of open and safe conversation without the fear of judgement or ridicule. I not only take care of but sincerely care for all of my patients. I have many single gay patients and a few that are in same sex marriages. I have seen an increase of gay married couples in my practice since the federal ruling legalizing same sex marriage in all fifty states. Many of my LGBT (lesbian, gay, bisexual, transgender) patients have voiced similar concerns over the years behind closed doors. They disagree with the legalization of same-sex marriages. Many secretly oppose "same sex marriage" but support "same sex union" sighting their Christian upbringing. One even prefaced her comments to me that she would never admit her views in front of "my gay friends". Many of my LGBT patients share that they believe their choice of lifestyle is morally wrong. They either love a particular person or a lifestyle too much to change. Either way it is misaligned love but only love conquers hate. There is no excuse or exception for violence targeted against a person's belief systems or lifestyle choices.

All forms of misaligned love set the hook of soul ties. Soul ties are deep seeded attachments that have apprehended and are trying to high jack your soul. Cindy Trimm offers an encouraging word in her book on spiritual warfare, "If you prevail in the Spirit, you will win in the natural. If you can learn the art of victory though intercession, then such struggles that steal the souls of humanity need not ever manifest at all." Many times soul ties are introduced by misaligned love or sexual sin. I provided care for a sharp and successful, beautiful young professional woman for several years. I was shocked when she had to be driven to my office because of incoherence. She was disheveled, depressed and defeated because of misaligned love. She was engaged to a man who loved and wanted to marry her. She was having second thoughts about marrying her fiancé. Her thoughts and her body had begun wandering back to a former lover. She intellectually knew that her ex was an ex for a reason. He had been abusive and unfaithful but she had a "place in my heart for him". She had a soul tie that was tethering her to her past. The young lady's past was keeping her from a future with her potential husband. Through prayer and acknowledgment of wrong mindsets, she requested the Lord to forgive her. She was delivered and able to commit wholly to God. She found wholeness in Christ. I John 1:9 says, "If we confess our sins, he is faithful and just to forgive us our sins, and to cleanse us from all unrighteousness." This young lady chose to remain single but is no longer tied to her past.

I enjoy fishing and one of the things you have to do when you get a bite is "set your hook". You must pull hard enough and at the right angle so the fish can't wiggle loose. The enemy has a way of setting the hook of sin in our souls. James Goll explains in *Deliverance from Darkness*, "Evil spirits chain people up, trapping them and holding them captive.

They make people into their puppets, to one degree or another." The devil can make feelings of condemnation, guilt, denial, rebellion and misaligned love hard to wiggle free from but I have some good news. Jesus came to set the captives free.

The Apostle Paul advises us in 2 Corinthians 6:14, "Be ye not unequally yoked together with unbelievers: for what fellowship hath righteousness with unrighteousness? and what communion hath light with darkness?". God is love. God is the Father of Lights and in Him there is not even the shadow of changing. God does not change nor does His Word. What was wrong for Sodom and Gomorrah is still wrong today. Rick Warren explains in his classic book, *Purpose Driven Life,* "You were made by God and for God-and until you understand that, life will never make sense. It is only in God that we discover our origin, our identity, our meaning, our purpose, our significance, and destiny. Every other path leads to a dead end." If two men walk and one falls one can help the other up. As believers, as children of light walking with the Lord we need to make a stand on the side of right. We should help lift our fellow man up out of the darkness created by the prince of this world. We do this by letting our light shine. There is no condemnation in Christ Jesus but by His Spirit we are set free.

**Mark 6:7** *And he called unto him the twelve, and began to send them forth by two and two; and gave them power over unclean spirits;*

# NOTES

# CHAPTER 3

# PERFECT LOVE THROUGH CHRIST

# PERFECT LOVE THROUGH CHRIST

**I John 5:7** *For there are three that bear record in heaven, the Father, the Word, and the Holy Ghost: and these three are one.*

The number three prophetically symbolizes the number of divine perfection. Jesus is perfect love and He is the Word of God made flesh. He is the living embodiment of God's love for humanity. God loved you and me so very much that He gave His only begotten Son to die in our stead. The wages of sin is death. Praise God that Jesus paid our sin debt while nailed to a cross on cavalry's hill. Colossians 1:17 says, "He is before all things, and in him all things hold together." Jesus is perfect love. He is the one who was, who is and who is to come. Jesus was before all things and He still holds all things together today. Jesus told the disciples that the first and great commandment is to LOVE God and the second is like unto it. We are to LOVE our neighbor as ourselves. Love God and love your neighbor as yourself because God is love. We are created in the image of a loving God and our actions, our lives should reflect that love. I grew up with as many of you probably did hearing, "love is what love does".

My home church hosted a reception honoring our members who were in their 90's. One of the women dedicated 70 years of service to not just that church but to the Lord. She thanked the congregation and pastor for giving them their flowers while they could still see and smell them. She said, "love is what love does" in her remarks.

1 John 4:20 reads, "If a man say, I love God, and hateth his brother, he is a liar: for he that loveth not his brother whom he hath seen, how can he love God whom he hath not seen?" Many apprehensible and hateful acts against our fellow, flesh and blood brothers are done in the name of a loving God. The skin covering our flesh might not be the same color but our blood bleeds the same shade of red. We all have hang-ups, preconceived notions and certain cultural biases. Many misconceptions stem from our upbringing and prior experiences. Jesus's love equips us to overcome our shortcomings. He is the true vine. Our righteousness should spring forth from Him.

Scripture reminds us that now we only see through the glass darkly. We often see our current situation through the clouded, dirty lens of our past. Only through the redemptive and cleansing Blood of Jesus can we be made clean. We must allow Him to renew our minds. I told the following story in *Fountain in the Valley*. When I first married I found a letter written to my husband from one of his old sweet hearts. I was infuriated by the contents of the letter. A few years later, after I had matured in the Lord, I again read the letter. There was nothing disturbing or inflammatory on the pages. The contents of the letter had not changed but the contents of my heart had. My mind had been renewed in Christ.

I was working in my office with the door closed a few years ago. I heard a new sales representative introducing herself to my receptionist. In a soulful and smooth Southern dialect the pharmaceutical sales woman sold her resume to the staff. She was attempting to meet with me face to face. The conversation consisted of telling the receptionist that we were in the same civic organization. The sorority consists primarily of socially aware African American women. I was intrigued by the dialogue so I put my paper work aside. At the waiting room window I SAW a beautiful, young Caucasian woman with eggshell shade, porcelain doll like skin. She had striking blue eyes and long straight blonde hair. I had to reconcile of my new sorority sister's voice

34

and persona with her appearance. My preconceived notions of race were challenged.

Over the next few years this lovely and loving lady shared her remarkable testimony. She described living a "mirage". She identified as African American despite looking Caucasian. Her African-American mother and Caucasian father were once deeply in love. They married and had a family despite being in the socially segregated South. Their love was tested by taunts and threats. The marriage soon crumbled and failed under the pressure of public scrutiny. Her father left his newborn baby and wife. His parents bribed him with the lucrative promise of a family inheritance if he would do so. My new sister in Christ tearfully told me of her childhood struggles. She inherited her father's light colored skin, hair and eyes. Her father left with a monetary inheritance. He never looked back to see the real treasure he left behind.

We see only now through a clouded glass. 1 Corinthians 13:10-12 reads, "But when that which is perfect is come, then that which is in part shall be done away. When I was a child, I spake as a child, I understood as a child, I thought as a child: but when I became a man, I put away childish things. For now we see through a glass, darkly; but then face to face: now I know in part; but then shall I know even as also I am known." Jesus is perfect love. He gives us the strength to live and love in an imperfect world. Doing what is right is not always easy but God's grace is sufficient. The abandonment of her father was especially difficult for her after the death of her mother. The young girl was taken in by and raised by her mother's sisters. She was moved further south to Mississippi. Their niece's appearance was a constant reminder of the betrayal of their baby sister by that "white man." This orphaned child was caught between two worlds. I am not referring to the worlds of black and white. She was caught between love and hate. This beautiful girl was the product of love but she often times did not feel that love. She grew up feeling mistrust and misgivings by the ones entrusted to love her. She was taunted and teased by cousins and classmates. A person cannot choose the skin they were born in. A baby does not ask to be born. We should love all this side of heaven's walls.

This young lady's upbringing and thus worldview was predominately African- American. Her physical appearance was Caucasian. She was caught in the dichotomy of her mother's love and her father's failures. She was given the nick-name "mirage". At a distance you saw her a certain way. As you get closer you see her inner truth and strength. I praise God that he allowed me to see my own biases through the mix of love and pain in her blue eyes. I was allowed to see the beam in my own eye and given a chance to remove it. God is so gracious. He orchestrates opportunities for us to see our own shortcomings. We have to see our faults in order to correct them.

I ran across an interesting analogy of an egg, carrot and coffee beans on Facebook recently. It compared what happens when each item was placed in boiling water. The egg was perceived as fragile initially. Upon removing from the heat it became hard on the inside and out. The carrot stick was colorful and vibrant before entering the hot water. It became soft and its color faded. In contrast the coffee bean's nature was consistent despite a challenging condition. It was steadfast but most importantly the bean changed its surrounding for the better. Likewise, we are to change our situations for the good. We are to be the light. Don't allow hot water nor difficult situations make you soft or harden your heart. You are to be the agent for change rather than allowing the situation to change you. My sister in Christ might have been considered a "mirage" because of the egg shell color of her skin early in life. Today her tenacity and inner beauty shows her true strength of character and loving heart.

We have all heard the old adage, you can't judge a book by its cover. I encourage you to not judge people by their physical appearance. Sometimes we have a gruff outer covering protecting a soft heart. Many have developed a protective layer because of past hurts but underneath they are beautiful. I had a vision a few years ago of marble stones that were different shapes, sizes and colors. They all had one thing in common. They were all beautiful. I heard in my spirit that that is how the Lord saw us. We all appear differently but we are "beautiful and strong." 1 Peter 2:5 confirms, "Ye also, as lively stones, are built up a spiritual house, an holy priesthood, to offer up spiritual sacrifices, acceptable to God by Jesus Christ." Our chips and cracks add to our character. A carnal man grades by a cookie cutter rating of cut, color and clarity. I challenge you to look a little deeper through the lens of God's perfect love. It is our uniqueness and diversity that makes us beautiful. Our beauty is seen when we allow seemingly incongruent pieces to fit together. In our individual brokenness we form a marvelous mosaic.

The words stretched and pressed were impressed in my spirit during a season of my life. The world tries to press you into their cookie cutter comfortable ideal. Their one-size fits all model does not work. We are all uniquely and wonderfully made. We are a chosen generation, a royal priesthood and a peculiar people. Identical twins may share the same DNA but even they do not have the same finger prints. The world attempts to press us into its mold. It tries to accomplish this through oppression. People try to suppress our uniqueness. Oppression and suppression of your purpose can lead to depression. God does stretch but He does not press. He will move us past our comfort zone. God encourages our growth. His Word is alive. When God's Word is alive on the inside of us then we grow. His Word is not stagnant nor should we be. As his children we should continuously grow in Him. Jesus is the True Vine and we are the branches. We can do nothing apart from Him but we can do all things through Him. *All through Christ: Christ through All.*

2 Corinthians 12:9-10 reads, "And he said to me, My grace is sufficient for you, for My strength is made perfect in weakness. Most gladly therefore will I rather glory in my infirmities, that the power of Christ may rest upon me. Therefore I take pleasure in infirmities,

in reproaches, in necessities, in persecutions, in distresses for Christ's sake: for when I am weak, then I am strong." We all have times of disappointments, setbacks and infirmity. God is God in the valley and God on the mountain high. I know this. I do speaking engagements and write books about this. I admit though that I was not feeling this. I was "feeling some sort of way" as one of the youngest members of our intercessory prayer team often laments. Don't get me wrong I was grateful and thankful for what the Lord had done in my life but I was tired. Within six months I had been diagnosed with a brain tumor. I was undergoing nauseating treatments and suffering from terrible headaches. I was coping with the death and the business of the burial arrangements of my father. All of this while starting a new clinic. I was hurting physically and emotionally. As a physician I was still ministering to God's sick and hurting people through my pain. *All through Christ: Christ through All.*

I was lonely despite being surrounded by people. I missed the routine despite the dysfunctionality of my prior practice. I was disappointed and demoralized by the health care and regulatory systems. I reported break-ins to my hospital owned practice. I was informed by the status quo that they had 1,100 other people to keep safe other than me. I was feeling "some sort of way". Hind sight is 20/20. I see now that the Lord was adding thorns to my nest. I had become too comfortable. Oftentimes if you have become comfortable in your current condition the Lord will add thorns to your nest. He is encouraging you to fly. He wanted me to go to the next level but I was holding on to mediocracy. God wanted me to Let Go. The last poem that I penned in this book is "Let Go and Let God". I know now that I was being stretched and prepared for God's best. The stretching did not feel good at the time but it was for my good. God is good. He is faithful and through it all, He is a Keeper. What the enemy meant for our harm God will make it for our good. I am healthier, wealthier and wiser. I have continued the tradition of providing compassionate and quality care to my patients. It is just now at a new practice location.

I love my patients and it is a privilege to be their physician. I honestly felt my purpose in Christ was being fulfilled by practicing medicine near my hometown. Luke 9:5 NLT reads, "And if a town refuses to welcome you, shake its dust from your feet as you leave …" I tried to make a difference but I found leadership to be indifferent. It is hard for oil to flow from the bottom to the top. I found that man is often tossed and turned as the tide changes. Men's opinions also may change as they listen to another's words despite seeing your works. Blustery winds of man's hot air can change a person's mind if they are not steadfastly secured in the good. God is good and in Him there is no shadow of changing. Corporations can be swayed by pennies rather than the best interest of people. Timothy writes that the love of money is the root of all kinds of evil. He continues that the love of money has caused many to wander from true faith. It has caused themselves many sorrows. Man's opinion may change but there is no need to wonder about God. In Him there is not even the shadow of changing. He is the solid rock. We should build our trust and hope on Him. Jobs and people change but God stays the same.

I was feeling disappointed and broken. Until God reminded me that I was whole in Him. I even requested the intercessors at my church to pray for my wholeness. I felt like a fraction of my former self. I had suffered so many losses in such a short period of time. I walked away from a full medical practice that I had spent the last decade of my life building. The practice was filled with not only 3000 patients but people who I considered friends. I wept and rejoiced with them. I celebrated at their weddings and mourned at their funerals. I cheered their triumphs and helped them find value even in their failures. I loved my practice and the souls the Lord had entrusted to me. I slowly accepted that this season was ending and my assignment had been accomplished. I rationally understood but understanding did not make my heart ache any less.

Within this short period of time my biological father died. My parents divorced when I was a baby. I was not afforded the privilege and blessing of my dad being in my home or life. Divorce divides not only the man and the woman but often leads to broken hearts and homes for many generations. But glory to God, the book of Isaiah says that Jesus is the repairer of the breach and the restorer of paths to dwell in. I was hurting and in my pain I was allotted the task of writing the obituary for a man I did not know. I attempted to reach out to him in my adult years with phone calls. Visits were unsafe because of his choice of lifestyle and living conditions. My childhood home was once filled with the sweet aroma of my grandmother's tea cakes and butter milk pies. Now it was filled with the deplorable stench of drugs and destitution. It is a horrible feeling to have a home but the inability to return to it. The house of my youth which was once overflowing with love deteriorated into a crack house. Drug addicts and dealers floating in and out dissuaded my visits. Chaplain Dr. Penny Njoroge writes in her book on healing from bereavement that when you lose a parent it is as if you are losing your past. I felt that my chance to help right the wrongs of my past died with my dad that autumn morning. But as my former pastor, Bishop Jim Lowe says, "life is choice driven and you live or you die by the choices you make." I had to come to grips that I had dedicated my life to ministering physical and spiritual wellness but my own dad died in a drug house. The quote, "Physician heal thyself" seemed to mock me during this dark period. I say on many speaking engagements, "I just practice medicine but God is the Healer." I knew that we all have a choice to make and a life to live but I still felt broken.

Jeremiah 31:28-29 reads, "And it shall come to pass, that like as I have watched over them, to pluck up, and to break down, and to throw down, and to destroy, and to afflict; so will I watch over them, to build, and to plant, saith the Lord. In those days they shall say no more, The fathers have eaten a sour grape, and the children's teeth are set on edge." I was hurting physically and emotionally. As the eldest child, I portrayed strength that I really did not have. In my brokenness I was led to my sister in Christ's church, Pastor Beverly Jackson. I praise God for His faithfulness. He placed on her heart just what I needed to hear that Sunday morning. Pastor Jackson pulled a twenty dollar bill out of her pocket during the sermon. She crumbled the currency and asked the surprised congregation if the crushed money still had value. She then reopened the twenty dollars and noted that the money was still whole and had value. This analogy symbolized us as believers. Many of us have been hurt but we can still find our wholeness and value in Christ. My wholeness was in Jesus's perfect love.

The three wise men navigated from the East to Jerusalem by looking up. They looked up and found the Son of God. Mathew 2:2 reads, "Saying, Where is he that is born King of the Jews? For we have seen his star in the east, and are come to worship him." Jesus is the way, the truth and the life. I encourage you my sister and my brother to continue to look up. Enter into worship of the Great I Am. Press pass your past and your hurts. Find your way in Him for He is The Way. Come up higher above treacherous betrayals. Look up and take the higher ground. Set your eyes on things above and stop focusing on the faults of others and your past regrets. Stop being led by emotions and by the longings for promotion. Be led by God's Spirit. Look to God. For eighteen years a woman was bent over until she met Jesus. She was bowed down and physically bound. Her spine was so deformed she was unable to see the beauty of a sunrise for eighteen long years. She was unable to look up for nearly two decades. As a physician I ascertain that the woman's likely physical diagnosis was kyphosis. She probably suffered from osteoporotic vertebral fractures. Her back bone became brittle and collapsed upon itself over time. This daughter of Abraham met Jesus. That same day her spine was made straight again. Jesus makes the crooked road straight. Just look up. Luke 13:12-13 reads, "And when Jesus saw her, he called her to him, and said unto her, Woman, thou art loosed from thine infirmity. And he laid his hands on her: and immediately she was made straight, and glorified God." This child of the King had been tormented by this tortuosity for decades. Immediately she was made whole. Who the Son sets free is free indeed. We must stop looking at the length of our affliction and the timeframe of our problems. We should only look up to the Ancient of Days who is our timeless Problem Solver. Jesus saw her and He had mercy on her. Jesus also showed mercy for the woman with the issue of blood.

The woman with the issue of blood had led a life of ostracism and criticism. Jesus prioritized her even though man treated her like a second class citizen. She pressed and pushed through the crowd to touch the hem of Jesus's garment. Jesus stopped everything and proclaimed that her faith had made her WHOLE. This woman found her wholeness in Christ and so can we. Be encouraged my sisters and my brothers. The Word of God says in 2 Corinthians 4:8-10, "We are troubled on every side, yet not distressed; we are perplexed, but not in despair; Persecuted, but not forsaken; cast down, but not destroyed; Always bearing about in the body the dying of the Lord Jesus, that the life also of Jesus, that the life also of Jesus might be made manifest in our body." I praise God that He has continued to allow me to be a beacon of His light in my new practice. I now have a position in the largest faith based hospital system in the country. God is good. He is Faithful and a Keeper.

Pastor Beverly Jackson used another anointed analogy in her sermon that Sunday. It also struck a chord with me. She described the events of our lives as the pieces of a quilt. They are all separate and compartmentalized but still interconnected. Our past is knitted to our present and forms our future. The pains of the lessons of the past should not be used to hinder or for excuses. Instead they should encourage growth. We should seek to grow from each lesson and testing like the rungs on a ladder or the steps on a stair case. Langston Hughes' poem summarizes this symbolism beautifully.

*Mother to Son*
*Well, son, I'll tell you:*
*Life for me ain't been no crystal stair.*
*It's had tacks in it,*
*And splinters,*
*And boards torn up,*
*And places with no carpet on the floor—*
*Bare.*
*But all the time*
*I'se been a –climbin' on*
*And reachin' landin's,*
*And turnin' corners,*
*And sometimes goin' in the dark*
*Where there ain't been no light.*
*So, boy, don't you turn back.*
*Don't you set down on the steps.*
*'Cause you finds it's kinder hard.*
*Don't you fall now—*
*For I'se still goin', honey,*
*I'se still climbin',*
*And life for me ain't been no crystal stair.*

During Jacob's night season God allowed Him to see angels ascending and descending upon a ladder. Even when we think we are at the end of our rope, God is faithful. If one door closes He will open a window. He promises not to put more on us than we can bear. Jesus came to bear the sins' of the world. We just have to cast our cares upon Our Lord and Savior because He truly cares for us. He will make a way out of no way and a *Fountain in the Valley*. Know that God is good and that He is working the situation out for our good. God is the god of another chance. He is faithful to forgive if we repent. Repentance is turning from our evil ways and returning to a loving Heavenly Father.

Dr. Martin Luther King's last speech, "I Have Seen the Mountain Top" was given at the age of 39 in Memphis's Mason Temple. It was a stormy night in the earthly and spiritual realm that fateful eve of his assassination. Jonas Clark in his book on spiritual authority eloquently summarized that night though not specifically writing about it. "The born again believer has been endowed with a delegated sovereignty both natural and spiritual. As the clash of kingdoms continues we can choose to respond in a number of ways. We can surrender, withdraw, compromise, be indifferent—or become Kingdom reformers. Kings have a grip on their purpose in life. They are willing to contribute to the greatest revelation of all time."

Dr. King, in his last appearance in a pulpit, prophetically referred to the Book of Amos. It reads "Indeed, the Sovereign LORD never does anything until he reveals his plans to his servants the prophets." Dr. King eerily ended his last public address with, "Like anybody, I would like to live a long life. Longevity has its place. But I'm not concerned about that now. I just want to do God's will. And He's allowed me to go up to the mountain. And I've seen the Promised Land. I may not get there with you. But I want you to know tonight, that we, as a people, will get to the promised land." God faithfully allowed Moses to look into the Promised Land prior to passing his mantle to Joshua. Apostle Jonas Clark writes in *Kingdom Living,* "Being a king means being at war with powers of darkness. No longer are we coming to church only to be blessed. We are getting blessed but we are also being trained as kings who understand the mandate of spiritual warfare to "put all enemies under His feet." Establishing Christ's Kingdom requires confronting and subduing the kingdoms of darkness. The pattern is found throughout Scripture. To possess means to occupy by displacing the former occupants."

Another portion of Dr. King's swan song speech that inspired me was on unity. We should show unity in Christ despite color or denomination. We should show determination to follow Jesus's mission of love despite deterrence. Dr. King wrote, "It means that we've got to stay together and maintain unity. You know, whenever Pharaoh wanted to prolong the period of slavery in Egypt, he had a favorite, favorite formula for doing it. What was that? He kept the slaves fighting among themselves. But whenever the slaves get together, someone happens in Pharaoh's court, and he cannot hold the slaves in slavery. When the slaves get together, that's the beginning of getting out of slavery. Now let us maintain unity … Let us rise up tonight with a greater readiness. Let us stand with a greater determination. And let us move on in these powerful days, these days of challenge to make America what it ought to be." I challenge all of us to look to Perfect Love, Jesus. He is our example of how to live a godly life even in ungodly situations.

I was recently led to re-read a book that was our first assigned reading in The School of the Prophets. The book, *A Tale of Three Kings*, is small yet powerful. It re-tells the tale of King Saul, David and David's son Absalom. The book recapped the relationship and rise to power of three kings from the same kingdom. After reviewing the manuscript and much meditation, I finally saw the relevance to us as students of the prophetic. We need to know ourselves before we can be trusted with the things of God. How a person handles adversity gives keen insight on how they will handle prosperity. Gene Edward's writes, "There is a vast difference between the outward clothing of the Spirit's power and the inward filling of the Spirit's life. In the first, despite the power, the hidden man of the heart may remain unchanged." Many followers of Christ want the fast track to becoming leaders but they despise even the thought of serving. We as followers of Christ should be servant leaders. Jesus washed His disciple's feet. He led by example. Many times we seek promotion without service. Often we want breakthrough but run from brokenness. We covet God's power but connive to avoid a contrite heart. We are often ungrateful when God does not move on our preconceived deserved grand scale. We turn coat if things are not done in our time table. Some dare to complain if the Maker of the Universe does not answer our prayers in our often array way.

Scripture warns us not to despise small beginnings. Jesus is our example of being a servant leader. The King of kings and the Lord of lords humbly knelt and washed the feet of His disciples. Jesus even washed Judas's feet. The Son of God washed the feet of the person He knew was plotting against Him. We all have Judas's or betrayers in our lives. We often time erroneously focus our attention on their wrongs. Rather than spending our time fault finding we should focus on Jesus's example of love. We should strive to become a servant leader. One of my favorite events that I look forward to occurs at the beginning of each year. The intercessors at my home church wash each other's feet. We prepare our hearts to pray for others by first seeking God to renew the right spirit within us individually and collectively. We humble ourselves and kneel and wash our sister's feet. It is a demonstration of love, humility and intimacy. John 13:11-16 reads, "For he knew who should betray him; therefore said he, Ye are not all clean. So after he had washed their feet, and had taken garments, and was set down again, he said unto them, Know ye what I have done to you? Ye call me Master and Lord: and ye say well; for so I am. If I then, your Lord and Master, have washed your feet; ye also ought to wash one another's feet. For I have given you an example, that ye should do as I have done to you. Verily, verily, I say unto you, The servant is not greater than his lord; neither he that is sent greater than he that sent him."

Christ instructs us to love our enemies and pray for those who persecute us. Jesus prayed for His Father's will and not His own. Matthew recounts Jesus praying with his face to the ground asking God, "O my Father, if it be possible, let this cup pass from me: nevertheless not as I will, but as thou will." Your will God and not mine. Your will Lord as it is in heaven. Let your will be in earth. Let your will be in our hearts and in our homes. Dr. Barry Cosper writes an inspirational and encouraging article entitled, "Just a Thought". It is published weekly in our local newspaper. Dr. Cosper applicably wrote, "Since God is everywhere, His rule and reign is everywhere throughout the created world. Even if you do not submit to His rule and reign, the kingdom of God still exists. If you resist the Spirit of God who is moving upon your heart, the kingdom of God will still exist and His will and purpose will still go forward." God's will is for us to be yielded and submitted vessels to Him. We are earthen vessels filled with heavenly treasures. God is the Potter and we are the clay. We are to be pliable to His purpose for our lives. We are only dust and from dust shall we return. A question remains. While we are planted on the earth will we pursue the Master's masterpiece for our lives or just play in the mud? Mud has been thrown at all of us. I warn that when we choose to wallow in pig stalls a passerby only sees dirty hogs. You can't tell in the middle of a fight who threw the first punch. Scripture advises us not to cast our pearls upon swine. We are to dust off our feet when the message is not received.

One of my favorite lines out of *A Tale of Three Kings* sums up the glorious goal of a broken spirit and a contrite heart. It encourages us to strive to humbly submit to God as His servant leader. It reads, "There in those caves, drowned in the sorrow of his song and in the song of his sorrow, David became the greatest hymn writer and the greatest comforter of broken hearts this world shall ever know." Without having passed through the valley of the shadow of death, I would not know for myself that God is a healer and a deliverer. A testimony is birthed out of a test. A true servant leader is birthed out of the pain of brokenness. 2 Corinthians 4:7-9 reads, "But we have this treasure in earthen vessels, that the excellency of the power may be of God, and not of us. We are troubled on every side, yet not distressed; we are perplexed, but not in despair; Persecuted, but not forsaken; cast down, but not destroyed." We once were lost but now we are found. We are broken to be made whole in Christ. His strength is made perfect in our weakness.

Servant leaders submit to the will of God not to the whims of man. I have found in my nearly two decades of medical practice the following lesson. I have had thousands of patients through my doors and have found that people are finicky. You are like a dog chasing its tail if you allow man or money to be your master. It is a never ending cycle of trying to please people who can't be pleased. Matthew 6:24 reads, "No man can serve two masters: for either he will hate the one, and love the other; or else he will hold to the one, and despise the other. Ye cannot serve God and mammon." Scripture encourages us to work in all things, even our secular jobs and schooling, as if working unto the Lord. Seek to please God and all other things will fall into place.

Jesus's Blood is still the same. It is powerful yet pure. It is strong but infused with saving grace. Much of our incongruence is that we believe God's grace is sufficient for us but is not sufficient for others. We pridefully feel others are not worthy of saving because of social, ethnic, racial, political, religious or gender differences. Jesus is the Rock and Chief Cornerstone but we must choose to allow Him to rebuild and restore our hearts. He is described as the stone the builders did not choose. He is the Beginning and the End. Jesus is all things to all men but they must believe He is. He is the Great I AM. I Peter 2:8 reads, "And a stone of stumbling, and a rock of offence, even to them which stumble at the word, being disobedient: whereunto also they were appointed." We all have hang-ups, preconceived notions, stereotypes and biases but we also have a choice. It is our choice whether or not to choose the light. We were all once blind. We all once thought our old ways were right. Scripture says when I was a child I thought as a child but when I became a man I put away childish things. I ask each of you to allow the Spirit of Truth to search your hearts and enlighten you to what childish things you need to discard. It might be jealousy, hatred, envy or strife. I feel that God is calling us up higher in unity and in love. Love never fails no matter how far you have fallen. Perfect love through Christ is the answer no matter the question.

One of the centurion soldiers who mocked, pierced and beat Our Lord and Savior saw the light. He saw Jesus at the shadow of the cross.

God's grace met him at the cross he had helped to erect. Matthew 27:54 expounds, "Now when the centurion, and they that were with him, watching Jesus, saw the earthquake, and those things that were done, they feared greatly, saying, Truly this was the Son of God." God will meet you at your need. No matter how far you have fallen His grace is sufficient. God is faithful to forgive. He stands at the door of our heart and knocks. He sends people to convict us. God pricks and primes our consciousness through His Holy Spirit so that we can see our short comings. He wants us to ultimately come into repentance. God's mode of operations is not condemnation. That hurtful and deceitful m.o. belongs to the enemy of our soul. Song of Solomon 2:4 describes how Jesus calls us with His love. It reads, "He brought me to the banqueting house, and his banner over me was love." God's banner over us is His love. God loved us so much that He gave His only begotten Son to reconcile us to His love. A holy and perfect God sent His Son to restore relationship to a sinful and damned mankind. Galatians 3:13 explains, "Christ hath redeemed us from the curse of the law, being made a curse for us: for it is written, Cursed is every one that hangeth on a tree:"

Love is what love does. Jesus gave His life for you and me so that even the people who crucified Him could be saved. Christ is our ransom. He is our propitiation from sin. My grandmother used to say that when you know better you do better. Dr. Barry Cosper blessed my heart with a quote from Pastor Warren Wiersbe. Pastor Wiersbe is known as "the pastor's pastor". This quotation helped re- shape my perspective of life and love during a season of transformation and restoration. It reads, "Truth without love is brutality, and love without truth is hypocrisy." During this pivotal point I was blessed with the opportunity and blessing to speak at a Mother's Day Tea where my mother and daughter were both in attendance. My scripture basis was 1 Corinthians 13:13 NLV, "Three things will last forever—faith, hope, and love—and the greatest of these is love." I retold a story from *Fountain in the Valley* of a mother's misaligned love. Her selfishness and drug addiction threatened her young daughter's physical and emotional well- being. This girl's "home" was a crack house. She was under constant threat of sexual exploitation and abuse. The child's focus remained on the only help she knew, God. This once spiritually barren mother attempted to trade her firstborn's virginity for drugs. But, God is a redeemer and answers the cries of His children. Through the mighty hand of God this entire family is now saved and serving God. They were also in attendance at this Mother's Day Tea. They testified with such unarming honesty. Their truth made many of the pearl wearing, tea sipping attendees uncomfortable. They told the crowd about their past pain and disgrace but in the same breath told of God's grace. The mother/daughter duet glorified God through their story of repentance and love. God forgave and restored this mother. That is amazing grace. The abused daughter who is now an adult chose to forgive and restore her mother.

God loves us too much to allow us to stay the same. Truth without love is brutality, and love without truth is hypocrisy. He wants to make our bitter into better. He wants to make our bigotry into bygones. He wants to transform our broken yesterdays into brighter tomorrows. Isaiah 61:3 reads, "To appoint unto them that mourn in Zion, to give unto them beauty for ashes, the oil of joy for mourning, the garment of praise for the spirit of heaviness; that they might be called trees of righteousness, the planting of the LORD, that he might be glorified." Jesus hung on a tree at Calvary so that we can be called His trees of righteousness. God is willing and able to save and to restore us. Are we willing to repent and make ourselves available to serve Him?

**1 John 5:7** *And there are three that bear record in heaven, the Father, the Word, and the Holy Ghost: and these three are one.*

# NOTES

# CHAPTER 4

# A FUTURE THROUGH CHRIST

# A FUTURE THROUGH CHRIST

**Daniel 3:25** *He answered and said, Lo, I see four men loose, walking in the midst of the fire, and they have no hurt; and the form of the fourth is like the Son of God.*

We are all familiar with the story of the three Hebrew boys, Shadrach, Meshach and Abednego. They defied the king, Nebuchadnezzar and refused to deny their Lord and King. Jesus is the King of kings and the Lord of lords. He promises never to leave us nor forsake us. Jesus was the fourth man in the furnace with His faithful followers. He was with them in the fire then and He is still with us now in our fiery furnace. Jesus had their back and He also has ours. He is still with us in our time of need. The Book of Isaiah describes God as our rear guard. Scripture also says that the LORD will go before us. He "got" our back and our front. Hallelujah, we can look to the hills which cometh our Help. We can move forward in Christ and walk by faith and not by sight. Our past can no longer hunt or haunt us because He "got" our back. Jesus has covered our previous mistakes with His Blood. We are covered by God's grace as we walk by faith into our futures.

As I toured, discussing *Fountain in the Valley* the topic that sparked the most discussion was from the chapter titled, "Bitter or Better". It was the testimony of a young wife and mother who had caught her husband in an indiscretion. She unwisely chose to fight fire with fire. My grandmother used to say if you play with fire long enough you will get burned. She had an affair despite knowing from her Christian upbringing that it was morally wrong. This young lady was living a double life. She was a faithful wife by day and a club hopping sorority girl by night. Soon after her wayward ways began, she developed severe headaches. After a thorough examination and imaging studies we concluded that her physical pain had its roots in a spiritual matter. I explain to my patients that even if they are mentally unwilling to admit stress that their body will often tell on them. I care for people working 80 hours a week on 4 hours of sleep a night, who verbally deny stress. Their exhausted bodies tell the tale with chronic pain and blood pressure elevations. They many times present with stomach ulcers, irritable bowel syndrome (IBS), tension headaches, migraines and elevated blood pressure.

You can't fix a spiritual problem with a physical solution, but you can fix a physical problem by spiritual means. Our God is a healer and a deliverer. This young wife and mother came to herself, repented and returned to her home. She became a fulltime wife and mother. Luke 15:18 reads, "I will arise and go to my father, and will say unto him, Father, I have sinned against heaven, and before thee," What is it that we need to arise from? What hidden sin has held us hostage? What person has held you in bondage? No matter what or whom has you bound, I know who came to set you free. Jesus came to set the captives free. Perhaps your sin is not adultery but scripture says that we all have sinned and fall short of the glory of God. Your sin might not be my sin but we all have sinned. We cannot afford to look down on anyone unless offering a hand up. I was privileged to speak at a Men's and Women's Day at a local church and my topic was, "We shall Rise". I encouraged the congregation from Proverbs that even though a righteous man falls seven times that he shall rise again. I am reminded of the poem, "And Still I Rise" by the late but never forgotten Maya Angelou. In part it reads, "You may trod me in the very dirt but still like dust, I'll rise." I was honored to tell this young lady's testimony at a church in the western area of Birmingham. I also shared with the congregation the story of the woman in the Bible caught in adultery. I explained how Jesus told the crowd that whoever was without sin should throw the first stone. I reminded the Sunday morning attendees that people who live in glass houses should not throw rocks. I then demonstrated how Jesus knelt and wrote in the dirt when the town's people came to accuse and stone the adulteress woman. She had been a mistress to many. God not only knew her sin but He knew who she did it with. When Jesus stood and looked around all of her accusers were gone. I told the group that Jesus stood up for this woman and He will stand up for us in our time of need. I asked the attendees if someone was "coming at" their loved one in the wrong way, if they would remain seated. The crowd unanimously answered, "NO". We unequivocally would stand to help our loved one and Jesus stands to help His loved ones. We are God's beloved. Jesus describes us as the apple of His eye. Jesus stood on earth for that adulterous woman and He stood in heaven for Stephen. Stephen was the first martyr of the Christian faith. People professing to be believers stoned him to death.

Often times the stones we face today are verbal accusations rather than physical assaults. They too, cause collateral damage and destruction when hurled. I have seen marriages and careers destroyed by untrue and unfounded words. Insinuation is a subtle yet effective tactic of the enemy. Insinuation seeks to divide, conquer and control through manipulation of buried emotions. Manipulation and controlling spirits are strongly linked to witchcraft. Scripture encourages us to watch and pray. Watch people who tell half the truth in order to prey on your emotions.

I have found myself caught in a war of words. A barrage of fiery darts were aimed in accusation at me and I recognized it was an attack on my reputation. The arrow that wounded me the most was when the people the enemy was able to enlist were friends and family. Workplace gossip might seem like casual conversations over the water cooler. Church house chatter is often seen as just catching up between choir selections until you and your family become the current discussion. I ministered to a group of women at a religious retreat about healing from the wounds of "church hurt". Certain places we feel are our sanctuary or safe haven. It is a place where we can put our guards down. The wounds inflicted in our "safe place" whether home or church often penetrate our hearts deeper.

I had a visceral response when I heard of the mass shooting at Emanuel A.M.E. Church in South Carolina. I was born, raised and currently reside in Birmingham, Alabama. Many knew "The Magic City" as "Bombingham" during the 1960's. This unflattering nickname arose then because of the rampant bombings of black homes, businesses and churches. Many people still have painful memories and heavy hearts because of the murder of the Four Little Girls and the bombing of 16th Street Baptist Church. Though they died 50 years ago when I heard of the South Carolina shooting I immediately thought of Denise McNair, Carole Robertson, Cynthia Wesley and Addie Mae Collins.

Pastor Clementa Pinckney and a few of the faithful parishioners of the majority black congregation of Emanuel A.M.E. church gathered for mid-week prayer and Bible study. The unthinkable happened again. Another mass killing occurred during an African American worship service. A Caucasian young male visitor was welcomed into Emanuel A.M.E's sanctuary. The members shared the Word of God and showed their unexpected guest the love of Christ before he perpetrated a heinous hate crime. Dylann Roof then a 21 year old opened fire and shot and killed 9 people including the pastor. He shot the church goers in their sanctuary at short range and in cold blood. Witnesses said that Roof calmly and calculatedly explained that he came to kill black people. The Dallas shooter callously crooned that he wanted to kill white police officers. I read on my radio show, What up Doc?, the week of the South Carolina church shooting Revelation 6:9-10. It reads, "And when he had opened the fifth seal, I saw under the altar the souls of them that were slain for the word of God, and for the testimony which they held: And they cried with a loud voice, saying, How long, O Lord, holy and true, dost thou not judge and avenge our blood on them that dwell on the earth? And white robes were given unto every one of them; and it was said unto them, that they should rest yet for a little season, until their fellow servants also and their brethren, that should be killed as they were, should be fulfilled." How long, O Lord? How long will people perpetrate hate in the name of heritage? Black lives do matter. White lives do matter. All of God's children's lives matter.

President Barak Obama, the 44th and first African –American president accepted the daunting task of performing the eulogy for Pastor Pinckney. President Obama's passionate address explained, "Our pain cuts much deeper because it happened in a church. The church is and always has been the center of African-American life—a place to call our own in a too often hostile world, a sanctuary from so many hardships. Over the course of centuries, black churches served as hush harbors where slaves could worship in safety; praise houses where their free descendants could gather and shout hallelujah—rest stops for the weary along the Railroad; bunkers for the foot soldiers of the Civil Rights Movements … We do not know whether the killer of Reverend Pinckney and eight others knew all of this history. But he surely sensed the meaning of his violent act. It was an act that drew on a long history of bombs and arson and shots fired at churches, not random, but as a means of control, a way to terrorize and oppress. An act that he imagined would incite fear and recrimination; violence and suspicion. An act that he presumed would deepen divisions that trace back to our nation's original sin." The past still seems to haunt and cause harm to our present. These horrendous murders occurred in a "sanctuary" in South Carolina. Our country's history records The Palmetto state as one of the last to end segregation. Reverend Pinkney served his congregation at Emmanuel African Methodist Episcopal Church and his community as a State Senator. His slain body respectably was laid in state inside the Columbia capitol building. This honor was bestowed after his procession passed, I feel disrespectfully, under the Confederate flag. It added insult to injury.

It begged the question hatred or heritage with the Confederate flag waving in the wind above the pastor's martyred body. The nation was again racially charged by more murders in yet another black church. United we stand and divided we fall. In a speech given in his father's home land of Kenya, President Obama said, "Recently, we've been having a debate about the Confederate flag. Some of you may be familiar with this. This was a symbol for those states who fought against the Union to preserve slavery. Now, as a historical artifact, it's important. But some have argued that it's just a symbol of heritage that should fly in public spaces. The fact is it was a flag that flew over an army that fought to maintain a system of slavery and racial subjugation. So we should understand our history, but we should also recognize that it sends a bad message to those who were liberated from slavery and oppression. And in part because of an unspeakable tragedy that took place recently, where a young man who was a fan of the Confederate flag and racial superiority shot helpless people in a church, more and more Americans of all races are realizing now that that flag should come down. Just because something is a tradition doesn't make it right." The pain of one of our members should be felt by all, if there is a true bond of brotherhood.

Black lives matter. White lives matter. Gay lives matter. Straight lives matter. We are all children of God. All of our lives matter. The worse mass shooting on U.S. soil was a hate crime targeted at homosexuals. Fifty lives were loss during a mass shooting in an Orlando gay night club. This was not just a crime against the LGBT community. It was a crime against humanity. A people divided cannot stand. The perpetrator of this horrendous crime was reportedly outraged when he saw a same sex couple kissing. Misunderstanding leads to fear which grows into hatred. Anger festers into rage. Many people fear what they do not understand. Beyond sexual preferences and beneath our skin colors people are the same. We all have sinned and we all are created in God's image. We should communicate with our fellow man in order to know our fellow man. Ignorance is not bliss. It is dangerous and volatile under the right circumstances. Not knowing breeds contempt and assumption. It is easier to believe a lie when you have never seen the truth. We are instructed to love our neighbors as ourselves. It is hard to love who you do not know. Knowledge is power. Only love dispels hate and perfect love casts out fear. Scripture reminds us that there is no fear in love but fear has torment. Strive to get out of your comfort zone of cushioned stereotypes. Seek to see people and not labels.

A person or group of people who do not know their history are doomed to repeat the mistakes of the past. Many discussions need to occur and these important talks should not be entered into begrudgingly. I recently attended a field trip with my son's elementary school class. We traveled by bus to Montgomery, Alabama and visited the Rosa Park's museum. There was a surreal reenactment of Mrs. Park's stance. She refused to yield her humanity by giving up her seat on the bus. This powerful woman who is called by many the mother of the modern civil rights movement penned a book entitled, *Quiet Strength.* She wrote in it regarding derogatory treatment, "After so many years of oppression and being a victim of the mistreatment that my people had suffered, not giving up my seat—and whatever I had to face after not giving up my seat—was not important. I did not feel any fear at sitting in the seat I was sitting in. All I felt was tired. Tired of being pushed around. Tired of seeing the bad treatment and disrespect of children, women, and men just because of the color of their skin. Tired of the Jim Crow laws. Tired of being oppressed. I was just plain tired." Enough is enough. When you learn better you should do better. An African proverbs says that once you learn then you should teach. Once you learn better then you should do better. We can teach through words but the best way to instruct is through our actions. We are enlightened to share the light with others. We are not shown the light to hide it under a bushel. We are to be the light of the world day in and day out. We are not to just shine our lights on Sunday mornings. Dr. Martin Luther King over fifty years ago said that the most segregated time in America is on Sunday mornings. A misconception is that time heals all wounds. That is untrue. If proper treatment is administered to the hurt then it can recover in a timely fashion. Love covers a multitude of sins. God is love and God not time heals all wounds. Allow the love of God to abound. Allow Him to heal our wounded hearts. A house, a nation and a church divided cannot stand. God is love and love never fails.

I have had to walk the road of healing with numerous patients after their homes were burglarized. The event might be long gone. The valuables might have been replaced but many still have a hard time regaining a good night's rest and peace. Jesus calls to all that are heavy laden to come to Him and that He will give them rest. We ultimately have two choices in this life. They are to have faith or be ruled by fear. Scriptures tells us that fear has torment. We should not let the fear of the past or questions about our future torment us. Instead we should walk out our present day in faith. Rick Warren writes in his book, *Purpose Driven Life*, "Many people are driven by guilt. They spend their entire lives running from regrets and hiding from shame. Guilt-driven people are manipulated by memories. They allow their past to control their future." My poem, "No Regrets" begins this manuscript and another one of my prophetic poems, "Let Go and Let God" ends it. I thank God that Jesus is the Beginning and the End. He is also our present help in our time of trouble. We should focus more on Jesus's face and not fear. We should focus more on our faith in God than on our fear of man. Hebrews 13:6 reads, "So that we may boldly say, The LORD is my helper, and I will not fear what man shall do unto me." People tried to persuade me not to write about terrorism or racial supremacists groups. They tried to instill fear into me. I chose to walk by faith and not live in fear.

We often watch our foes from a distance but welcome our friends and family into our "safe place". Often the line between friend and foe is blurred when Christ is no longer the focus of the relationship. Jealousy is truly a green eyed monster. This evil spirit distorts the truth and seeks to divide. Many can no longer see or appreciate their gifts because they are comparing what God gave them to what others have. They can't utilize their gift because they are too busy wasting useful time looking at what the Jones' have. The book of Hebrews encourages us to focus and fix our eyes on Jesus who is the perfector of our faith. He alone is our refuge and peace in the storm. Jesus is the one to be praised, worshipped and adored. The prize is not a person, place or position. We should press toward the prize of the high calling of God in Christ Jesus.

The LORD is our ever present help in our time of trouble. His Word promises that no weapon formed against us shall prosper. These scriptures allude to the fact that we as believers will have trouble and weapons will form. Praise God that all things will work out for our good in the end. While writing *Fountain in the Valley* I admittedly was in a valley season. I have not publically shared the details of my struggle until *All through Christ: Christ through All.* James 1:2-4 reads, "My brethren, count it all joy when ye fall into divers temptations; Knowing this, that the trying of your faith worketh patience. But let patience have her perfect work, that ye may be perfect and entire, wanting nothing." Proverbs tells us that warning comes before destruction.

I had a dream about two women at the beginning of my two yearlong dilemma. This ordeal prompted me to leave my medical practice. The two women in the dream were grotesque and wore revealing lingerie. I dreamt that they leisurely strolled into my bedroom and made themselves VERY comfortable in my bed. There were other people "in bed" with them and several others standing and watching the travesty. In the dream I was unable to make the devilish duo leave or gain assistance from the onlookers. I then left my bedroom to find one of the previous observers telling the tale to a captive audience in my kitchen. This dream was a warning from the Lord of things to come. My actual medical practice a couple of weeks after the dream was broken into by two women. People who I never would have suspected where in cahoots with the robbery. Many people who I trusted in my inner circle were only there to fan the flames of gossip.

In this difficult season of life, God taught me the difference between reputation and character. I learned that reputation is what people think about you but character is what God knows about you. My friendships were tried and only the true ones remain today as pure gold. Job 33: 15-18 NIV reads, "In a dream, in a vision of the night, when deep sleep falls on people as they slumber in their beds, he may speak in their ears and terrify them with warnings, to turn them from wrongdoing and keep them from pride, to preserve them from the pit, their lives from perishing by the sword." The dream did frighten me. I was unsure what the Holy Spirit was trying to convey to me. I prayed and sought guidance from the Spirit of Truth. John 16:13 NLT says, "When the Spirit of truth comes, he will guide you into all truth. He will not speak on his own but will tell you what he has heard. He will tell you about the future."

I had noticed a few small things missing from my office around this time. On other occasions items seemed to be in different places rather than where I had left them. I notified management, security and even filed a couple of police reports. The authorities did not initially take the complaints of a busy doctor with a messy desk seriously. It was just papers that were missing. They assumed that I had just misfiled or misplaced them. The dream was still in the forefront of my thoughts so I installed cameras in non –patient care areas. Authorities were later surprised to see two ladies on surveillance video leaving my office. The robbers looked to me as if they were carrying my prescription paper in their hands. The district attorney did not agree. She said the print was too small to clearly see the RX on the blue and white watermarked paper. The mannerisms of the burglars matched the women in the dream but no one seemed to know who the women on the tape were in real life. The plot thickened but the enemy's plan became clearer. I began receiving phone calls from pharmacies near and far regarding forged prescriptions for controlled medications on this blue and white RX paper.

The state where I practice ranks number one in the nation for the worst prescription painkiller addiction and diversion problem. The pushers are peddling prescription narcotics as well as the street opioid heroin as an alternative to cocaine. Heroin use among our youth is skyrocketing. Overdose rates from narcotics have quadrupled in the past decade. The face of an addict is beginning to look like the suburban "girl next door". Most heroin users report starting out using then subsequently misusing prescription medications. They then progress to harder drugs for cheaper and stronger highs. With most businesses whether or not legal or illegal it is a matter of supply and demand. The increased street demand for prescription medications has caused a rise in robberies of doctors' offices and pharmacies. One of my colleague's medical practice was burglarized three times in one week before the culprit was caught.

A five year illegal drug operation involving pharmacy employees at a Georgia hospital was exposed and halted recently. The pharmacy technicians from 2008-2013 allegedly put around 30 million dollars' worth of narcotic pain pills and cough syrup on the street. Literally, surveillance cameras captured the accused wheeling crates of controlled medications down Peachtree Street in Atlanta. The article reads, "Emory Midtown's case is yet another example of how prescription drugs can be put to illegal uses at top brand-name hospitals, even when administration think they're following the rules. There are no statistics on how often these kinds of cases happen, in part because the hospitals hush them up … they let problem employees go quietly and fail to report the thefts to law enforcement and regulators …" Over a million pills each of hydrocodone with acetaminophen and Xanax, plus over

100 gallons of promethazine with codeine were carted out of the back door of this hospital. These drugs are now on our streets. These hospital employees fueled the drug epidemic in the same community they were supposed to be servicing. Often administrators will turn a blind eye to avoid leakage of possibly detrimental stories. They seek to protect their company's reputation while harming the community as a whole.

Who is protecting the good of the community? I brought up issues of suspected drug diversion to a hospital administrator and was told they had 1,100 other people to protect. 1,100 was the number of people that the community hospital employed. But, what about the other 26,000 residents in a community where overdoses have quadrupled and homicides are way to common place? Luke 15:4 reads, "What man of you, having an hundred sheep, if he lose one them, doth not leave the ninety and nine in the wilderness, and go after that which is lost, until he find it?" A good shepherd protects all of his sheep and will even go out of his way to maintain his flock. John 10:12-13 read, "But he that is an hireling, and not the shepherd, whose own the sheep are not, seeth the wolf coming, and leaveth the sheep, and fleeth: and the wolf catcheth them, and the wolf catcheth them, and scattereth the sheep. The hireling fleeth, because he is an hireling, and careth not for the sheep."

I then took my complaints and suspicions to the DEA and State Pharmacy Board. I might be considered a whistle blower but I am no one's scapegoat. I offhandedly remarked to the lead detective that I could write a book about my ordeal. He responded, "You should make it fiction because no one will believe it." Jesus is the Good Shepherd. The Pharmacy Board in response to my reports has issued written warnings to several local pharmacists. The pharmacists were accused of dispensing controlled medications under fraudulent circumstances. The state legislative branch is now investigating as well. Many good people have been adversely affected by this prescription drug epidemic.

An elderly pharmacist who had dedicated his career to our community was shot in the back and robbed while locking the door of his family owned business. In another incident within the same year another pharmacist was charged with Medicaid fraud. Both pharmacies are located in a city that has a population of less than 30,000 people. This city despite its small size was listed as one of the country's most dangerous cities. The fraud charge came about when allegedly, the pharmacist and mother of a sick child conspired. They billed Medicaid for medication which was never actually purchased or distributed. The terminally ill child never received his treatment. The parent and the pharmacist allegedly shared in the proceeds from the insurance pay out.

Sometimes there has been a fatal intercession between the healing art of medicine and crime. The oath to do first do no harm has become a suggestion. Sadly, honesty and integrity have become exceptions to the rule. There are unscrupulous individuals in all walks of life but I expect more from health care professionals. I personally know great doctors who have dedicated their lives to their individual patients and the improvement of their communities as a whole. Unfortunately, people who earn the right to wear white coats do not always have the right character. Wearing a white coat does not equal having a right heart. People might recite an oath to serve and protect or first do no harm but many make these pledges for selfish ambition. They have become self-serving rather than servants of mankind. Money, power and success are often great manipulators of even a strong man's morals. A television sports commentator when discussing sports in the U.S. said that some coaches would recruit Hannibal Lector if he could score. 1 Timothy 6:10 reads, "For the love of money is the root of all evil: which while some coveted after, they have erred from the faith, and pierced themselves through with many sorrows."

Local news reported laptops, prescription paper and lists of doctors DEA numbers were confiscated during raids on "drug houses". State and federal officials joined resources in an operation called "pilluted". More than 22 doctors and pharmacists were arrested in 4 Southern states over a 15 month time span. Some doctors were accused of trading prescriptions for money and /or sexual favors. Pharmacists were investigated for dispensing controlled medications without physician authorization and for ill gained profit. The medical profession and the pharmaceutical field have been unfortunately polluted. A culture of addiction has been cultivated in our country by a few rotten apples. Zephaniah 3:1-3 reads, "Woe to her that is filthy and polluted, to the oppressing city! She obeyed not the voice; she received not correction; she trusted not in the Lord; she drew not near to her God. Her princes within her are roaring lions; her judges are evening wolves; they gnaw not the bones till the morrow."

After the before mentioned dream my real life became a nightmare. I began to receive calls about forged prescriptions in my name from pharmacies in and out of state. I was even threatened in my clinic exam room by a new patient when I refused to write narcotics for his back pain. This drug seeker I was later told carried a cane as a prop to gain sympathy from doctors. When his ruse did not work with me he threatened me with it. He slammed the cane on the exam room table. I never thought while in medical school that my then dream job would involve filing police reports.

The culture of physician patient relationships has been detrimentally affected by professional con-artists who prey on doctors. The patients who are truly in pain are suffering the greatest because of the lack of doctors willing to provide proper analgesia. I became not only concerned for my livelihood but for my life. I never imagined that entering into the healing arts that I would be afraid for my physical wellbeing. No one ever said a gun license would go hand in hand with a medical license. I have been threatened and literally chased from a hospital room while on call. An HIV positive, drug addict lunged at me after I refused to provide her fix. Her drug of choice was intravenous Dilaudid.

Most parents would be proud if their child showed a desire to pursue a career in medicine. I instead cautioned my children against their potential medical career goals. I admit that I attempted to dissuade my daughter's aspiration of being a Pre-Med major. I literally and figuratively had to place my burdens of fear and anger upon the altar. Perfect love casts out fear and Jesus is perfect love. Matthew 6:25-26 reads, "Therefore I say unto you, Take no thought for your life, what ye shall eat, or what ye shall drink; nor yet for your body, what ye shall put on. Is not the life more than mean, and the body than raiment? Behold the fowls of the air: for they sow not, neither do they reap, nor gather into barns; yet your heavenly Father feedeth them. Are ye not much better than they?"

After noticing odd things out of place in my office I proactively placed hidden cameras in public areas. The police were unable to identify the woman so I took it to a higher a source. I placed the picture on the altar during our weekly prayer meeting. The previously unidentifiable woman on the video came forward within a week of giving my cares to the Lord. Prayer does work. A local media outlet picked up the story of the break-in from the police's Facebook page. Seeing her picture on the evening news coaxed the lady from my dream to pay a visit to the police station. John 16:8,13 read, "And when he is come, he will reprove the world of sin, and of righteousness, and of judgement:", "Howbeit when he, the Spirit of truth, is come, he will guide you into all truth: for he shall not speak of himself; but whatsoever he shall hear, that shall he speak: and he will shew you things to come."

One of the intercessors spoke a rhema word during a powerful Wednesday prayer meeting. She said that the horse and the rider would perish in the sea. This word applies to this situation because a slang term for a person who transports drugs is a drug mule. The woman was clearly walking out of my office with my prescription paper in her hand. She was caught on camera red handed but no arrests were made. Authorities said that the trail drew cold when witnesses would say that they were afraid for their lives to share further information. Psalm 76.6 reads, "At thy rebuke, O God of Jacob, both the chariot and horse are cast into a dead sleep." God tears down the house of the proud but establishes the house of the humble. My hope and my help is in the Lord. He opens doors that no man can close. He also closes doors for the protection of His children. He is the Light of the World and praise Him for shining a light in my dark situation. What the enemy meant for my harm I thank God for turning it around for my good.

Another intercessor during this anointed mid-day worship service warned of wickedness in high places. A horse has to have a rider much like a drug mule has to have a leader. Ephesians 6:12 reads, "For we wrestle not against flesh and blood, but against principalities, against powers, against the rulers of the darkness of this world, against spiritual wickedness in high place." God knows and He holds the heart of the king in His hand. He can turn it either way He chooses. The truth will prevail. The horse and the rider will fall into the sea. Many of my patients wondered why I relocated my practice across town and associated with a different hospital. Much speculation and allegation have been brought to my attention during my transition. I hope this book offers answers to these lingering questions. Scripture says that your gift will make room for you and I am currently affiliated with one of the largest faith based hospital systems in the country. I can now share my faith and pray with my patients. I no longer fear ridicule or risk of retaliation. My practice of medicine has always been a ministry. It highlights that God is the Healer and we as physicians only practice medicine. Some of us get it right and others do not.

The intercessory prayer leader at my home church often warns us not to make prayer meeting into an opportunity for "holy gossip". We often purposely withhold painful details of prayer requests to avoid the temptation of tattling tongues. People who live in glass houses should not throw stones. There is an unsuspected shattering of trust when the stone is thrown from under your own roof. We are a church "family". We are the Body of Christ. If one part of our physical body hurts then we all should feel the pain. 1 Timothy 5:12-13 read, "Having damnation, because they cast off their first faith. And withal they learn to be idle, wandering about from house to house; and not only idle, but tattlers also and busybodies, speaking things which they ought not." Scripture also says that love covers a multitude of sins. That covering of love does cover betrayal. Jesus was betrayed by Judas and He still lovingly washed his feet. If feelings of betrayal are left unchecked they can develop into a root of bitterness. Roots and weeds can destroy a garden no matter how beautiful it appears.

Prophet Joni Ames warned against a spirit of division at a recent prophetic meeting. She cautioned that this conniving spirit was trying to destroy our country, churches and families from within. Many of us have great security systems to defend from an attack from without but how well do we handle an attack from within? Jealousy is not just a powerful emotion but it is a spirit that tries to infiltrate the ranks. Envy often stems from an erroneous air of entitlement that spreads through idle and insidious words. Reports of violence at political rallies are rampant on the news and social media. We are one country. United we stand but divided we fall. We are made up of many unique parts that make up a strong whole. Our beauty is found in unity but our ugliness is shown in division. Our nation's great sin is slavery. Hate mongering and divisive language will not make our nation great again. We are to learn from our mistakes or we are doomed to repeat them. I am solemnly reminded of the black and white news reels from the sixties as I view the current evening news. History shows that divisive rhetoric directed at particular ethnic and religious groups causes civil unrest and confusion. God is the author, finisher and perfector of our faith. God is not the author of confusion. My grandmother used to say "There is a way to do things" and this is not the way. Our nation's strength is found in acceptance and inclusivity not fear. It was not found then in Bull Conner's water hoses nor will it be found in political rallies that end in a melee. Love never fails. Perfect love, Jesus casts out fear. Jesus promised to not leave us comfortless. He left His believers the Spirit of Truth who will guide us into all truth. Our future is found through Christ.

I have been so blessed by the testimonies of comfort and faith that book chat participants from *Fountain in the Valley* shared. One gathering was in a small southern town, with a majority Caucasian female attendance. We initially began discussing a snow storm that paralyzed the city a few years ago. An elderly lady shared how an African-American man had to hold her arm to steady her gait across the iced sidewalk home. She was appreciative and in need but admitted that she was uncomfortable being that close to a Black man. Startlingly to the group an African- American woman in her 60's interjected an incident. She described how she was flagged down in her 4-wheel drive SUV by a Caucasian man stranded on the side of the road during the same storm. The listeners were shocked to hear that she was afraid to pick up this well dressed middle aged white man. She told the group that she did eventually give the stranger a ride. On the way to his home she realized the stranger was actually her neighbor. People are not that different. The common thread should be love and compassion and not hate and distrust.

Another story was shared in a small town's library. They invited me to speak during the anniversary of the tornado locals named, "April's Fury". It had been five years since the town's largest known natural disaster. I am also a disaster relief chaplain. We were discussing God's faithfulness during the storm. A tearful woman interrupted with details of a near death situation. Minutes after the F-5 tornado hit a husband and wife made their way through the rubble that was once their home. They were frantically looking for their two children. They found their young son about 20 feet away from the home. The blustery winds had blown the boy but the search party soon found him alive though with fractured bones.

They then turned their attention to looking for their teen age daughter, "Hailey". Neighbors and family yelled her name until the mother stumbled upon her unconscious and bloody body. They began to weep and pray kneeling beside Hailey's lifeless body. The child suddenly opened her eyes. Their daughter told the stunned onlookers that she was just at the most beautiful place. Hailey said she saw many other neighbors there. She saw Mr. and Mrs._____ there, too. The couple told Hailey to tell everyone that they decided to stay there. Later that evening Mr. and Mrs._____ bodies were found. They died in the storm. Hailey went on to say that she did not want to return either. The place was so beautiful with its pure, clear and blue light. Hailey heard her mother calling her name and decided to come back. The effectual and fervent prayers of the righteous avails much. Hailey's grateful family after the storm erected a sign where their house once stood. It read, "Jesus saved us. Ask Him and He will save you, too". God is faithful. He is a Savior.

No matter how the winds of life blow or the stones people throw Jesus will never leave us. Jesus will not forsake us. He was in the storm with Hailey. He was the fourth man in the fire with the Hebrew boys. The power hungry ruler threw the young men into the fiery furnace. These boys had a strong backbone because they refused to bow and worship the statue erected in King Nebuchadnezzar's honor. No matter your stature, title or degree one thing is for sure; every knee shall bow and every tongue shall confess that Jesus Christ is Lord. It is your choice whether to bow willingly or unwillingly. It is your choice whether to bow today or tomorrow but every knee shall bow. Every person will see Him as King of kings. God's will shall show forth. It can either happen the easy way or the hard way but every knee shall bow.

King Nebuchadnezzar saw the 4th man in the fire. The idol building, boy burning ruler, witnessed the pre-incarnate Christ protecting His children. He saw Jesus walking with His servants in the midst of the fire. The three Hebrew boys were thrown bound into a furnace. King Nebuchadnezzar had ordered it heated seven times hotter than normal. Two of the king's servants were burned to death while placing the Hebrew boys in the oven. In contrast not a hair was singed on God's servants' heads. The fourth man, Jesus, appeared at His servant's time of need. Nebuchadnezzar saw through the flames and smoke four men walking unbound within the fiery furnace.

Glory to God, Jesus came to set the captives free. When Jesus comes on the scene no matter what has tried to bind you or how strong the bond has been it has to bow. The three Hebrew boys exited the fiery furnace unbound, unharmed and not even smelling like smoke. Jesus set the captives free. God changes not and nothing is impossible with Him. God set them free and Glory to God He is still willing and able to set us free. He can deliver us from whatever attempts to bind us. It does not matter if the captor is drugs, addiction, adultery or fornication. God is our deliverer. He is also not a respecter of persons. If God did it for them I know He will do it for me, too.

Scripture warns to touch not His anointed and to do His prophets no harm. The Ten Commandments clearly instruct us not to make any graven images. We are not to bow down nor serve any other god. Jehovah is a jealous God. Every knee shall bow but they shall bow at the name of Jesus. Every tongue will confess that Jesus Christ is Lord. King Nebuchadnezzar learned this lesson but he learned it the hard way. He called for Daniel after God released the three Hebrew boys from the furnace. Nebuchadnezzar had a worrisome dream about a big and bountiful tree that was cut down to a stump. Warning comes before destruction. Daniel warns that the tree represented the king's kingdom and it will be cut down. Every knee shall bow, even the knee of the king. King Nebuchadnezzar not only bowed his knees but he walked on all fours for seven years. Daniel 4:33 reads, "The same hour was the things fulfilled upon Nebuchadnezzar; and he was driven from men, and did eat grass as oxen, and his body was wet with the dew of heaven, till his hairs were grown like eagles' feathers, and his nails like bird's claws."

The mighty king once built a huge monument in his own honor. He had a majestic palace but now he wandered the woods with no roof over his head. The whole kingdom once bowed to his image whenever the musicians played. Now, he was bowed down grazing on grass with the beasts of the field. He was so powerful that people danced to his beat as his musicians played. Now his feet are as claws. God is our Keeper if we realize it or not. King Nebuchadnezzar eventually acknowledged God as God. He repented of pride and his mind and kingdom were restored. Elohim is the Keeper of our mind. He alone gives us peace.

I often tell my patients struggling with disobedient children or spouses gone astray that God is a keeper. The caveat to this is that we have to want to be kept. Away from God we only have a piece of our mind not peace of mind. God is our maker and He is our mind regulator. Pride does come before a fall. The higher you have allowed people to place you the harder the fall from their pedestal. King Nebuchadnezzar learned his lesson on brokenness while living seven years in the wilderness like a wild beast. Daniel 4:37 reads, "Now I Nebuchadnezzar praise and extol and honor the King of heaven, all whose works are truth, and his ways judgement: and those that walk in pride he is able to abase." Every knee shall bow and every tongue shall confess that Jesus Christ is Lord. Every knee, no matter how high it started out will bow. Scripture tells us to humble ourselves before the mighty hand of God. We must seek to submit to His will and humble ourselves before He has to humble us. Every knee shall bow including yours.

Every knee shall bow including the knees of sickness and disease. We have a future through Christ. Around eight months ago I began having episodes of headaches and dizziness. I have faith in the Great Physician but God gave us earthly doctors and resources to maintain our health. A MRI showed a brain tumor. As King Hezekiah did in the Bible days, I turned my face to the wall and I prayed. I sought a second opinion from the Most High God and I believed His Word. I heard the words, "disappearing acts" during prayer. I was recommended to a specialist who started me on twice a week treatments. I diligently adhered to the medical regimen but I also believed God for His, "disappearing acts". I was awaiting the 6 month follow-up MRI to ascertain treatment success. A long term patient came in with a similar medical dilemma. She had been given the diagnosis of a brain aneurysm after an abnormal imaging study for headaches. I adjusted her hypertensive medications and added a cholesterol medication. I treated her physical condition. I was also led to share with her the word the Lord laid on my heart, "disappearing acts". I prophesied to her in the midst of waiting for my repeat MRI that her test and mine would be negative for the Glory of God. While you are waiting for your miracle what words will you confess? Whose report will you believe? I will believe the report of my Lord, Savior and King. I asked the radiologist on call to read my repeat MRI of the brain in my presence. My colleague asked what he was looking for because he did not see anything abnormal. I explained the test was to follow-up a brain tumor, he answered, "What brain tumor?". Glory to God. A few days later the young patient had her repeat imaging study. No aneurysm was found and she is now headache free. Who the Son sets free is free indeed.

Prophet Joni Ames, one of my mentors in the prophetic ministry, teaches that we are to wage war and stand in faith with the prophetic words that the Spirit of the Lord gives us. I clearly heard, "disappearing acts". I stood on that word and in faith shared that word with my sister in Christ as the Spirit gave utterance. God is faithful and He is not a respecter of persons. If He healed us then He will heal you, too. Hebrews 2:4 reads, "God also bearing them witness, both with signs and wonders, and with divers miracles, and gifts of the Holy Ghost, according to his own will?" We have a future through Christ.

**Daniel 3:25** *He answered and saith, Lo, I see four men loose, walking in the midst of the fire, and they have no hurt; and the form of the fourth is like the Son of God.*

# NOTES

# CHAPTER 5

# GRACE THROUGH CHRIST

# GRACE THROUGH CHRIST

**Luke 9:16** *Then he took the five loaves and the two fishes,
and looking up to heaven, he blessed them, and brake,
and gave to the disciples set before the multitude.*

The number five prophetically symbolizes God's grace. God's grace is His unmerited and undeserved favor. He bestows His grace lovingly on mankind. The wages of sin is death but God in His mercy and love gave us His only begotten Son. Jesus died in our stead. Jesus the Lamb of God fed the hungry multitude then and He still is Our Bread of Life today. Jesus is the ultimate and final sacrifice. Isaiah the prophet writes, " …saith the LORD: I am full of the burnt offerings of rams, and the fat of fed beasts; and I delight not in the blood of bullocks, or of lambs, or of he goats." Christ sacrificed His life for ours. The Son of God shed His blood on Calvary's cross as a propitiation for our sin. Jesus is God's grace personified and personalized. Jesus is available to be our Personal Savior if we accept His gifts of grace, salvation and sacrificial love. Freely He gives but freely we must receive. Jesus freely gave His life so that we may have eternal life but God also gives us freewill. It is our choice to accept or deny God's grace. His grace was given through the shed Blood of God's Only Begotten Son. Jesus warns us that whosoever denies Him before men He will deny before His Father. Jesus is the way, the truth and the life. Jesus is The Light of the World. He is the only way to The Father.

Jesus's grace includes salvation. He in addition mercifully purchased our peace that surpasses all understanding, healing and deliverance. He came to set the captives free from whatever or whomever has them bound. Jesus delivers us, His beloved. He delivers us from the bondage of ungodly mindsets, sickness and disease. Jesus proclaimed in the synagogue more than a thousand years ago, "The Spirit of the Lord is upon me, because he hath anointed me to preach the gospel to the poor; he hath sent me to heal the brokenhearted, to preach deliverance to the captives, and recovering of sight to the blind, to set at liberty them that are bruised." Jesus then announced that that day the scripture had been fulfilled. Jesus still beckons for the lost. His call of grace and freedom shines in the darkness like a beacon of light and hope. Jesus is the Hope of Glory and He personifies the grace of God. Pastor T. D. Jakes in his book *Life Overflowing* explains, "Grace is the attitude of God that causes His love to transcend our sin and deliver to us the full measure of His support and work. Grace means that we don't have to strive and struggle through this life in oppression or depression because God has given us favor. His grace is what enables us to move forward and run the race with confidence---without shame or condemnation---because we know His love is unconditional."

God is our way-maker and He provides for us. We are not in this world alone. His strength is made perfect in our weakness. I have been privileged to host several book chats on *Fountain in the Valley*. I discerned early on that this forum provided people a platform to discuss experiences they had previously shied away from sharing. One of these events was at Pell City, Alabama Public Library. The attendees were from a local book club and literary group. I was explaining that the origin of *Fountain in the Valley* was a dream. An elderly woman then began recapping a dream that she had in previous years. She still remembered it in amazing detail. The lady vividly described to the group her dream about Jesus. She retold how Jesus was standing on a jagged rock surrounded by a raging sea. He was bending down and extending His hand to a young man who was sinking in a storm. The drowning man had on tattered and frayed clothing. The weather worn and weary man saw Jesus standing on the rock. He desperately reached out to grab Jesus's nail pierced hand. The pensive woman recollected the look of concern and care in Jesus's eyes. She relayed to the crowd the firm grip the Savior had on the young man's hand. Jesus pulled him to safety. Mark 1:41 reads, "And Jesus, moved with compassion, put forth his hand, and touched him, and said unto him, I will; be thou clean." Jesus still saves. Jesus still delivers. Be still and see the salvation of the Lord. He is our Savior and friend.

The book chat attendee said that when she awoke she knew the dream was to become a painting. The caveat to her revelation was the lady did not know how to paint. The elderly widow was also on a limited fixed income. She could not afford to commission an artist. Jesus is the Way Maker and the woman was a willing vessel. Months after the dream the woman was attending another event at Pell City library. Not by accident but by divine orchestration the door prize for the event was for a commissioned oil painting. The woman registered gleefully. She knew this was the way her dream would become a reality. Her beautiful piece of art now hangs in her church's foyer. She donated her winning to a local church. She wanted the story and picture to be shared with God's people. Jesus is the Way. The Lord gave this faith filled woman a dream. He then made a way for the dream to come into fruition. We simple must have the faith of a mustard seed and believe. Performing the miracle is God's responsibility. Be encouraged nothing is impossible with God.

I had a vision while encouraging a young lady to continue in her passion and calling. I saw what looked like an entrance to a mall's department store. The entryway was pressure sensitive. There was a weight sensing sliding glass door entryway. As the woman of God walked toward the closed door it opened automatically when she reached a certain spot. We should walk by faith and not by sight even. Never stop walking even, if what we see before us is a closed door. God's grace meets us where our need and faith intercede. We have to press toward the mark of our high calling in Christ Jesus. Allow God's grace to work on your behalf. He will shatter man's earthly imposed glass ceiling and open up the windows of heaven. Instead of moving forward in God's grace and His enabling power we often resist His assistance. Many of us fight the process and refuse to walk in grace. We refuse to submit and often fight God's will.

An alternative scenario is of a revolving door of greasy grace rather than the glorious open door of God's grace. Some slip, dip and tip but cry out for mercy when they are caught in their wrongdoings. Many back-slidden believers know the gospel but they choose to willfully submit to sin over and over again. The Apostle Paul warns of this cyclical life of sin. People wrongfully use God's grace as a scapegoat. Dr. Barry Cosper further explained in his weekly newspaper devotional, "However, the reason we often find ourselves going back to every idol, addiction, bad habit and negative behavior that has haunted and shamed us in the past is because we do not replace it with that which is of God. We become legalistic and proud about what we are not doing, while quietly struggling along, trying to do the things of God without the power." Like in the iconic board game we "pass go" only to regress to the beginning. We have to begin again and again because of mistakes, misdeeds and misdirection.

Pastor David Weir, who is senior pastor at Victory Christian Church preached three steps on how to keep your heart free from sin. He advised the congregation to first admit our sins. We all have sinned and fall short of the glory of God. God is faithful to forgive if we confess our sins. Secondly, Pastor Weir instructed us to submit to God. Scripture says that if we submit to God and resist the devil that the enemy will then flee. Lastly, we were reminded to focus on God. Many soldiers of the faith lose heart by focusing on the enemy rather than keeping their eyes fixed on Jesus. Jesus is the author and finisher of our faith. He is the ever present help in our time of trouble. The battle was not David's when he fought Goliath. It was then and still is the Lord's battle. David focused on his faith in God and not on his fear. He was able to defeat his giant and we can overcome whatever giants that are in our lives. We overcome the enemy by the Blood of the Lamb, the word of our testimony and not loving our lives to the death. God was with David and He is still with us, now. We must admit our transgressions then submit to God. Focus on God and not on the giant. Focus on God's strength and not on our weaknesses. Focus on God's power and not the prowess of your foe. Romans 6:14-15 reads, "For sin shall not have dominion over you: for ye are not under law, but under grace. What then? Shall we sin, because we are not under the law, but under grace? God forbid." God's word is to be a lamp to our feet and a light to our path. He leads us in the paths of righteousness and to victory.

I first met the woman who God allowed me to encourage through the vision of the automatic door when she was a child. As a teenager I watched her parents carry her adorned in lavish lace and ruffled dresses into church. They would then gently place her on a front row pew atop a pillow. I was in awe when the adorable yet disabled child was handed a microphone. Her angelic voice blessed the congregation. As a physician I now understand the whys behind the delicate and gentle treatment of the pretty little girl with the anointed voice. She was born with a bone disorder called osteogenesis imperfecta. In laymen's terms she has brittle bone disease. This beautiful and brave woman entered the world with thirty-five broken bones. All of them were from the trauma of exiting the birth canal. She beat the odds and continues to press toward the mark. Despite the inability to walk and the limited function of her arms she still sings for the glory of God. In my vision as in life she moves forward in faith. She overcame her physical ailments. She is a prayer warrior and minister of the gospel. She is an active intercessor at her church. She navigates the aisles in an electric wheelchair to encourage the sick, weary and brokenhearted.

God's grace is sufficient but we must press toward the mark. Don't stop or settle for second best. We must step out in faith. Pastor T.D. Jakes writes in his book, *Life Overflowing,* "Grace is also the power that enables us to endure and progress through insufferable challenges ... We can never forget that what God has called us to do is beyond our abilities, talents, and strength. Consequently, God infuses us with His divine enablement, the supernatural energy to do superhuman exploits for the kingdom." The Apostle Paul writes in 2 Corinthians 12:9-10, "And he said unto me, My grace is sufficient for thee: for my strength is made perfect in weakness. Most gladly therefore will I rather glory in my infirmities, that the power of Christ may rest upon me. Therefore I take pleasure in infirmities, in reproaches, in necessities, in persecutions, in distresses for Christ's sake: for when I am weak, then am I strong."

We as believers are given the divine opportunity to proclaim God's grace and mercy through our testimony. Scripture reminds us that we overcome by the Blood of the Lamb, by the Word of our testimony and not loving our lives to the death. I was blessed with the chance to minister to the American Heart Society's Circle of Red. I am a spokesperson for the American Heart Association and a guest blogger. I discussed that particular evening how heart disease is the number one killer of women nationwide. Cerebrovascular related deaths surpass even the top three cancers of lung, breast and colon combined. I debunked the notion that heart disease is a man's disease and taught the deadly truth. Heart disease claims the life of 1 in 3 women. My two mentors allowed me to share their testimonies of survival from heart disease at the gathering. Pastor Beverly Jackson was in attendance. I explained that after reporting her symptoms to her primary care physician that she was sent home. An EKG nor blood work were performed. She was young and active so he assumed her symptoms were not heart related. She suffered an acute myocardial infarction later that week. The D in the GO RED slogan is "Don't Be Silent." Her testimony will prayerfully encourage other women to seek medical attention. We should also pursue and persist to find an answer for any unresolved symptoms. Don't be silent.

I encouraged the group of working mothers and wives gathered for the Circle of Red soirée with a Bible passage. I discussed when the disciples asked Jesus what is the Greatest Commandment?. The Master told them to love God with all their heart, soul and mind. He went on to explain to His followers that the second is to love your neighbor as yourself. We show love for God and our fellow man but often neglect our own physical health. There has to be a balance between spiritual and physical wellbeing. You can't successfully accomplish all of God's purpose for your life without taking care of yourself. I Corinthians 6:19-20, read "What? know ye not that your body is the temple of the Holy Ghost which is in you, which ye have of God, and ye are not your own? For ye are bought with a price: therefore glorify God in your body, and in your spirit, which are God's." I encouraged the women who excelled at maintaining multiple irons in the fire to take the time to care for themselves. I posed the question of how many of them take their cars in for service regularly but neglect going in for their yearly physicals. We must strive to show love to God, our fellow man and to ourselves. It is not selfish to take time to exercise, prepare a healthy meal or get ample sleep. I have discerned two main tactics of the enemy aimed at believers who are on the right path. The deceiver will try to lull them to sleep with a spirit of indifference or alternatively push them too fast. He wants to tire them out before their purpose is accomplished. Finding balance in Christ is key. Jesus is the Good Shephard and He leads His sheep and His sheep know His voice. God doesn't drive us like a herd of cattle but He leads us tenderly with His still small voice. Jesus promised not to leave us comfortless. The Holy Spirit leads and guides us in all truth. He is the light to our path. He makes the crooked way straight for He is the Way, the Truth and the Life.

Scripture recounts how Jesus and His disciples ministered to the needs of the multitudes but at the end of the day, they broke away to a desert place to rest. The Bible gives several accounts of Jesus taking time away to rest. If Jesus, the Son of God took the time to rest shouldn't we? In this particular setting the groves of spiritually thirsty people pushed through and positioned themselves to be fed by the Master. Much like the story of the woman at the well they sought life giving water. John 4:14 NLT reads, "But those who drink the water I give will never be thirsty again. It becomes a fresh, bubbling spring within them, giving them eternal life." The crowd sought living water in a desert from the Giver of Life. Jesus still provides for us today even in a parched and dry land. No matter how hard our heart has become or unfertile our lives seem Jesus is able to saturate and restore. Jesus is still our *Fountain in the Valley* and our well spring of life in the desert. Isaiah 41:18 reads, "I will open rivers in high places, and fountains in the midst of the valleys: I will make the wilderness a pool of water, and the dry land springs of water." Jesus did not turn the hurting and broken hearted away but instead He healed them.

One of the most spiritually challenging times of Jesus's ministry occurred on the Mount of Olives specifically in the Garden of Gethsemane. Earlier that evening Jesus partook in the Last Supper with his twelve disciples. He revealed that one of them would deny Him and yet another would betray Him. After Jesus washed His disciple's feet this fateful night He prophetically broke bread and dipped it in wine. This represented His soon to be shed blood on the cross for our sakes. He then took three of His most trusted and closest followers, Peter, James and John to go intercede for Him. The time which He had been born for was drawing near. Jesus prayed intensely and intently to His Heavenly Father about the cup passing by Him in the Garden of Gethsemane. The cup symbolized the death on the cross. Scripture says that Jesus was only a stone's throw from His disciples while He cried out to the Lord. He prayed so passionately that His tears became as blood. Jesus instructed His faithful few to also be in prayer. Luke 22:40-42 reads, "And when he was at the place, he said unto them, Pray that ye enter not into temptation. And he was withdrawn from them about a stone's cast and kneeled down, and prayed, Saying, Father, if thou be willing, remove this cup from me: nevertheless not my will, but thine, be done." Jesus returned twice to find His followers sleep on the job. Soon after Jesus's prayer time, Judas entered the garden. He was accompanied by a blood thirsty mob. Judas came to betray the man who earlier that night had washed his feet. Judas betrayed the Son of God with a kiss. Jesus promised to never leave us nor forsake us and to stick closer than any brother. He "got" our back even when we don't have His. Jesus was just a stone's throw away from the drowsy disciples even in His time of tumultuous temptation.

I was blessed to witness Jesus's stone's throw away grace. I was speaking at a women's Christian weekend conference. The setting was a beautiful lakeside setting nestled in the mountains. One of our exercises on receiving God's forgiveness for our iniquities and freeing others from their transgressions included writing our aught on a white stone. We then prayed, forgave and prophetically cast the rocks that had held us bound into the lake. Scripture instructs us to cast our cares upon the Lord because He cares for us. Just as with disciples in the Mount of Olives, Jesus is only a stone's throw or prayer away. Revelation 2:17 reads, "He that hath an ear, let him hear what the Spirit saith unto the churches;"To him that overcometh will I give to eat of the hidden manna, and will give him a white stone, and in the stone a new name written, which no man knoweth saving he that receiveth it." Jesus is our heavy load bearer and allows us to become a new creature in Him.

A group of ladies at the retreat had been standing in prayer with each other for a heavy burden. They were led by the Holy Spirit to write their prayer petition on a large boulder. Neither one of the women could carry the rock to the shoreline alone. Together they heaved what had weighed them down into the water. The faith filled believers were disappointed to see the stone sink in the lake with a large splash only a few feet in front of them. They were not strong enough even with their joint effort to hoist the rock any further. The Word of the Lord reminds us in Zechariah that not by might nor by power but by the Spirit of the Lord. The dismayed ladies then witnessed a miracle of God's grace. The stone miraculously rose from the muddy and murky water and skated across the lake as far as their eyes could see. Psalm 40:2 NIV reads, "He lifted me out of the slimy pit, out of the mud and mire: he set my feet on a rock and gave me a firm place to stand." This story reminds me of the miracle of the ax head. Elisha's disciples went to the woods to clear more land for a larger dwelling place. While working their ax fell in the Jordan River. Elisha in a prophetic act cast a piece a wood into the water. The ax then rose and was retrieved. With God All things are possible.

To assist us to prepare in prayer for the participants of this weekend retreat one of the event leaders, Tara Bensinger wrote a 33 daily devotional. Our day 5 meditation topic was prophetically on grace. Tara wrote, "The enemy wants us to believe that we are not good enough for the love of Father God. The father of lies wants to steal our understanding of the truth that we are coheirs with Christ and deeply loved by the Bridegroom. The truth is that we are indeed the Bride of Christ, in whom He delights. His love and desire for us is passionate and personal. He created us for companionship and relationship. He deeply loves us. I remember the very day I heard the message of grace for the first time. It was then that the gap between me and that far off God seemed to dissipate. Suddenly, He became closer. And as I began to walk in grace, He became intimate. Personal. Grace has radically changed my life. Because of grace, I now have an intimate relationship with Abba, my Father and friend. The lover of my soul and my very heartbeat. Grace is what brings me to my knees, time and time again. Grace has truly set me free." I praise and thank God for His grace embodied in His Son, Jesus. Freely He gives. Freely we must receive.

No man or woman is an island. Part of God's grace for our lives are relationships that He ordains and arranges. We are given the beautiful assignment to maintain these friendships. Friends are the flowers in the garden of life and whatever you feed and nourish will grow. Our Master purposefully intertwines our lives with other members of the Body of Christ. Part of our journey is to pause long enough to see who is planted on either side of us. We are more similar than we many times admit or acknowledge. If we don't step out of our comfort zones we can isolate ourselves. We think our bubble of safety is protecting us but often it is only blocking our blessings and development.

God also showered me in His love as I volunteered to serve. He showed me His grace at this mountain top Christian retreat. I was ministering through my brokenness. I was selected to give a talk on godly leadership. Few knew that I was struggling with the recent diagnosis of a brain tumor and the death of my biological father. During a worship service a young lady whispered in my ear, "Your Daddy, God loves you." I was encouraged and moved to tears. I was studying the term Abba, Father. This rhema word of my Father's love brought the logos word back to my remembrance. Abba is the Arabic word for father. It is used in scripture a handful of times. The term denotes an intimate relationship between a child and his father. It loosely translates to our term of endearment, daddy. God is Our Heavenly Father. We are saved by grace so that no man can boast. Galatians 4:5-7 reads, "To redeem them that were under the law, that we might receive the adoption of sons. And because ye are sons, God hath sent forth the Spirit of his Son into your hearts, crying, Abba, Father. Wherefore thou art no more a servant, but a son; and if a son, then an heir of God through Christ." Jesus also addressed God as Abba Father in the Garden of Gethsemane. Jesus asked His Father to remove the cup from Him but in the same breath He submitted to His will. God's grace is sufficient and His mercy is everlasting. God's will is not always painless but it is always perfect.

A human rights and health travesty occurred on U.S. soil. The cause was dirty water and even dirtier politics. Flint, Michigan is an economically struggling, majority African-American city. High lead levels were detected in the drinking water and in the city's residents.

Institutional racism was first defined by Sir William Macpherson who is a retired high court judge in the UK. The U.S. and the UK are divided by the sea but in reality they are not that far apart. The British Judge wrote this response to the racially motivated murder of a black youth named Stephen Lawrence who was killed on the streets' of London. Judge Macpherson defines institutional racism in his dissertation. It reads, "The collective failure of an organization to provide an appropriate and professional service to people because of their color, culture, or ethnic origin." Lead was allowed to leach from the pipes in the aging infrastructure of a 57 % black U.S. city. The events started when state government voted to change Flint's water source in an effort to save money. Money was saved but unfortunately lives were lost. Black lives do matter. Poor lives do matter. All lives do matter. This environmental debacle is an example of institutional racism. God is not a respecter of persons regardless of color, culture or ethnic origin. Mathew 25:40 reads NIV, "The King will reply, "Truly I tell you, whatever you did for one of the least of these brothers and sisters of mine, you did for me."

There have been ten deaths in Flint, Michigan from Legionnaire's Disease since the switch from Lake Huron to the Flint River for their water supply. Legionnaire's Disease is a rare but often fatal bacterial infection that can cause death by pneumonia. Legionnaire's Disease is transmitted by contaminated drinking water. It usually effects immunocompromised people with underlying lung disease such as COPD (Chronic Obstructive Pulmonary Disease). Epidemiological studies usually show outbreaks in hotels and hospitals rather than in whole cities. Our political leadership's mandate should be to serve and protect. They should especially strive to protect the ones unable to protect themselves. This travesty disproportionately affected the sickest among us and our young.

The parents and even the children's pediatricians complained. The policymakers turned a deaf ear to their cry. A courageous and astute physician noticed the trend of rashes and increasing blood lead levels in her patients. She reported her findings in 2014 but the issues were not addressed until 2016. This young doctor was the light in darkness. Dr. Mona Hanna-Attisha attempted to turn the bitter water sweet with the truth. Moses was directed by God in the wilderness to dip the branch of a tree in the bitter water. It became sweet and sustained the Children of Israel. This Old Testament reference of the tree foreshadows Jesus's death on the cross. The death on a cross is bitter. It is written in the Bible that cursed is any man who hangs from a tree. Jesus died a bitter death but He is sweet I know. Jesus took the sting and bitterness out of death for us. We as Christians are called to share this living water and truth not only in our homes. We are to share the truth in our communities. John 16:13 reads, "Howbeit when he, the Spirit of truth, is come, he will guide you into all truth: for he shall not speak of himself; but whatsoever he shall hear, that shall he speak: and he will shew you things to come."

Lead poisoning can be insidious and can cause neurological and psychological maladies. It has been linked to learning disabilities, ADHD and seizures years after the initial exposure. The risk is greater when nutrition is poor. Lead poisoning disproportionately affects the poor amongst us. Lead likes to imitate and mimic calcium. When there is a calcium deficiency then high lead levels predispose to anemia and kidney disease. This is tragic but the tragedy does not end with the directly exposed generation. Lead can effect reproductive organs. Its affects can be seen in the next generation.

A national state of emergency was issued. Residents of Flint received federal assistance. It still begs this question, though. How did city and state government so fail their frailest citizens? Scripture says that warning comes before destruction. The elected city government was replaced by a governor appointed city manager prior to the lead debacle. The new city manager declined to add an anticorrosive agent to the city's water supply. The new regime decided to save some dollars rather than treat the lake water with the recommended anticorrosive agent.

The cost for the treatment would have been about one-hundred dollars a day. What is the cost of a life? Lives matter. People matter whether they are black, white, rich, poor, old or young. Matthew 18:5-6 reads, "And whoso shall receive one such little child in my name receiveth me. But whoso shall offend one of these little ones which believe in me, it were better for him that a millstone were hanged about his neck, and that he were drowned in the depth of the sea."

God is a loving God but He is also a just God. I marched with my teenage daughter through the streets of downtown Birmingham protesting the murder of Trayvon Martin. We walked the same route the foot soldiers took decades ago. We echoed the battle cry of the civil rights advocates' decades before us. We chanted, "No Justice, No Peace" after the murder of another African American teenager. Trayvon had committed no crime. He was walking home after purchasing an evening snack from the neighborhood store. The young man was a person of color in a majority Caucasian Florida community. He became the person of interest of George Zimmerman. Zimmerman was the self-nominated one-man neighborhood watch. He lethally shot the unarmed teenager. Trayvon's only crime was walking while being black. Zimmerman was acquitted of Trayvon's murder. Zimmerman has been involved in various domestic disputes and had many arrests since the deadly shooting. Trayvon did not have a criminal record but his body now rests in a casket. George Zimmerman is now horrifically trying to profit from his horrible crime. He is attempting to sell on-line the weapon that he used to kill an un-armed youth.

Sureshbhai Patel was excitedly visiting the United States from India for the first time. Unfortunately, while vacationing in America he was racially profiled. The senior adult was assaulted by police while going for a leisurely midday stroll. The father was visiting his son's home in "Sweet Home Alabama". Similar to Trayvon's case a neighbor called 911 and reported a black male walking through his community. The person specifically told police that a "skinny black man" was in his exclusive neighborhood. The officers of the law arrived to investigate. The non-English speaking elderly gentleman could not answer the officer's questions to their satisfaction. He had arrived in the U.S. only two weeks prior to the incident. Police proceeded to throw the 57 year old grandfather to the ground face first. The man's neck was broken and he remains partially paralyzed. The victim's only crime was walking while being a person of color. The case against the police officer was dismissed. Justice should have no color. Our men in blue should serve and protect even the black and brown citizens. They should not make innocent people black and blue with bruises. Citizens should respect the law and law enforcement. We are all people if we have a badge or not. We all bleed red and have a family we want to return home to.

I admit my bias. Two of my high school memories embedded a distrust for our judicial system. I remember as a teenager the horror of hearing of my uncle's ordeal with Birmingham Police. My uncle faithfully served our country and is a decorated Marine veteran. He survived the war but was brutally beaten by police during a traffic stop after returning home. He was punched repeatedly in the face. His eye was enucleated. In laymen's terms his eyeball had to be removed because of the blunt force trauma. Later in the same year a personal run in with local law enforcement tainted my senior prom. Customarily so, my escort and I were dressed in our finest array. On our way to our celebratory milestone we were stopped by a policeman. We were detained at a stop sign for "stopping too long". The officer then proceeded to pick an empty beer can from the side of the road. He then falsely accused us of throwing the container out of our vehicle. Our only crime was driving to a black tie event while black. We were not arrested but we were harassed. We arrived at our prom late but my view of the world changed early.

Justice should be for all and not just for the rich and powerful. Presidential candidate and former Secretary of State Hilary Clinton said in a campaign speech, "We have to begin facing up to the reality of systemic racism, because these are not problems with economic equality. These are problems with racial inequality." God is a just God and He is not a respecter of persons. Justice shall prevail. Psalm 37:28 reads, "For the LORD loveth judgement, and forsaketh not his saints; they are preserved for ever: but the seed of the wicked shall be cut off."

Moses's name means to draw out of the water. His mother placed him afloat the Nile River in a basket. She submerged him among crocodiles and snakes in an attempt to save his life. We are still among cold blooded predators but God still protects. Moses was born during the time of an edict declared by Pharaoh. He commanded the midwives to kill all the Hebrew male babies. But, Glory to God that He retains a remnant. Puah and Shiphrah were midwives who refused to go along with Pharaoh's genocidal ploy. Moses's mother, Jochebed bravely hid her son in an attempt to save his life. Pharaoh's plot was to murder masses of slave boy babies because the captives began to outnumber the free. Pharaoh instituted this evil plan to maintain power and control. Moses's mother and the midwives had to walk by faith and face the fear of disobeying an unfair law. Dr. Martin Luther King wrote in his letter from a Birmingham jail, "One has not only a legal but a moral responsibility to obey just laws. Conversely, one has a moral responsibility to disobey unjust laws." God still retains a remnant today. It is our choice to either go against the erroneous status quo or go with the flow of wrong. Isaiah 10:22 reads, "For though thy people Israel be as the sand of the sea, yet a remnant of them shall return: the consumption decreed shall overflow with righteousness."

During a national prayer conference call in early 2012 we were praying for God's will in the upcoming presidential elections. I heard in the spirit and I shared with the participants on the line the words, "Forward March". On April 30, 2012 President Obama's campaign announced that its slogan would be "Forward." The Lord allowed me to know the winner of the election prior to the votes being cast or counted. I also heard rhema word in the spirit regarding the 2016 Presidential election. I am sharing it for the first time publically in *All through Christ: Christ through All.* During prayer I was led to the following scripture. Jerimiah 31:22. KJ It reads, " How long wilt thou go about, O thou backsliding daughter? for the LORD hath created a new thing in the earth, A woman shall compass a man." I foresee that we will have our first woman president in the United States of America. There is a time and a season for everything.

A news reporter only reports the news. They do not write or change it. Likewise, they do not necessarily agree with it. I am only reporting what I hear in the spirit realm. God sent Noah to Nineveh with a message of destruction. The people not only heard the word but they repented because of it. There is power in prayer. Nineveh was spared by a gracious God. 2 Chronicles 7:14 reads, " If my people, which are called by my name, shall humble themselves, and pray, and seek my face, and turn from their wicked ways; then will I hear from heaven, and will forgive their sin, and will heal their land." I have been appalled by some of the legislation passed down by U.S. courts in the last fifty years. Sexual sin has been legalized. Murder has been legitimized into a choice. The marital bed has been profaned. Even though something is made the law of the land, it is still not necessarily the Law of God. We are to serve a higher power. Man cannot serve two masters. We are to choose this day who we will serve. We cannot expect a holy and pure God to bless our unrighteous and dirty hands. Isaiah 1:18-20 reads, "Come now, and let us reason together, saith the LORD: though your sins be as scarlet, they shall be as white as snow; though they be red like crimson, they shall be as wool. If ye be willing and obedient, ye shall eat the good of the land: But if ye refuse and rebel, ye shall be devoured with the sword: for the mouth of the LORD hath spoken it."

Pope Francis also weighed in on U.S. politics after his visit to Mexico. He said, "A person who thinks only about building walls, wherever they may be, and not building bridges, is not Christian." Scripture charges us to show love for the aliens or immigrants for we were once aliens in the land of Egypt. Charity starts at home then spreads abroad. Aliens can be our modern day new co-workers or transfer students. Character is how you treat people who you assume can offer you nothing in return. Be good to God's people and watch God be good to you. The good works that you do in private, God will reward you publically for them. The dirt people dish in the dark and sweep under the rug will be uncovered. Take care of your character and God will take care of your reputation. The Book of Hebrews encourages us to show hospitality to strangers. There is grace through Christ and grace in Christ. We must show God's grace to receive His grace. Grace, mercy and forgiveness are reciprocal. Matthew 6:14 reads, "For if ye forgive men their trespasses, your heavenly Father will also forgive you:" The Bible explains that we might have even entertained angels unknowingly. Jesus admonishes us to feed the hungry, care for the sick, visit the prisoners and take in the strangers. The phrase, "What would Jesus do?" became popular in the 1990's. This term might be cliché but it still holds credence today. I ask, "What would Jesus, do?" I once gave a lecture to a group of Pre-Med college students. The title of the talk was "The I.T. factor". I encouraged these intelligent future physicians to always place their Integrity before their Talent. Talent will take you far but integrity will keep you there.

During one of President Barak Obama's speeches given from Kenya he chronicled his grandfather's life. Our president's granddad was a domestic servant in Africa for the British. President Obama shared painful details from his grandfather's life while visiting his ancestral homeland. His grandfather even as a grown man with children of his own was still referred to as "boy". It is God's grace that the grandson of a servant could become president of the most powerful country in the world. Scripture warns in Proverbs that the earth cannot bear when the servant becomes king. There is a season for everything. President Obama's given name, Barak, means blessed in African. Scripture reminds us in the beatitudes that blessed are the persecuted for theirs is the kingdom of God. Blessed is the grandson of a servant. Ecclesiastes

3:1-2 reads, "To everything is a season, and a time to every purpose under the heaven: A time to be born, and a time to die; a time to plant, and a time to pluck up that which is planted;"

The battle is not ours but it is the Lords. Our job is to seek and submit to God's will. Zechariah 4:6 reads, "Then he answered and spake unto me, saying, This is the word of the LORD unto Zerubbabel, saying, Not by might, nor by power, but by my spirit, saith the LORD of hosts." The battle is not ours but we do have a vital role to play. We have to walk in faith and not in fear. The enemy is a defeated foe. We simply have to walk the process out. The road was not promised to be easy but God does promise to make the crooked places straight. Jesus is the author and finisher of our faith. He is the beginning and the end. Jesus knew our end before our beginning. Our job is to stay close to the author and finisher of our faith. We then allow Him to direct us in His ways. He is the way, the truth and the life. We simply have to follow Our Leader.

Scripture says in John 10:10, "The thief cometh not, but for to steal, and to kill, and to destroy: I am come that they might have life, and that they might have it more abundantly." No matter what the enemy's plans are they are null and void per the Blood. Old Testament believers were directed to place the blood of a lamb above their doors. This prophetic act marked God's territory. The death angel had to pass them by. We still today as Christians are covered by the Blood of the Lamb, Jesus. God's Holy Word confirms that no evil shall befall us nor any plague come near our dwelling. God is our refuge still today. He gives His angels charge over us. Elisha's servant was frantic because the enemy had surrounded their camp. The prophet prayed that the lad's eyes be opened. His servant was able to see the legions of angels that were protecting their dwelling place. Psalm 91:10-11 reads, "There shall no evil fall thee, neither shall any plague come nigh thy dwelling. For he shall give his angels charge over thee, to keep thee in all thy ways." I plead the Blood of Jesus and ask for Psalm 91 protection daily over me and mine. I recite with my children Psalm 23 and 91 as we wait at the school bus stop each weekday morning. The Holy Word of God directs us to train up our children in the way they should go. When they are old they will not depart from it. Our most important job as parents is to train our children in the ways of God. My pastor, David Craig urges us often on Sunday mornings to keep our main thing the main thing. The main thing should be a solid personal relationship with the Rock of our Salvation.

The Word of God is described as the sword of the Spirit. A sword like God's Holy Word is an offensive and a defensive weapon. We can cover our families offensively with His Word by: pleading the Blood of Jesus, asking for God's Psalm 91 covenant of protection and by placing the whole armor of God on them. The armor of God is described in Ephesians chapter six. It includes the belt of truth; the breastplate of righteousness; the shoes of peace; and the shield of faith. God's Word is also a defensive weapon. Hebrews 4:12 reads, "For the word of God is quick, and powerful, and sharper than any two-edged sword, piercing even to the dividing asunder of soul and spirit, and of the joints and marrow and is a discerner of the thoughts and intents of the heart." The Word of God which is the sword of the spirit is our defensive and our offense. Jesus is the Word of God and the grace of God made flesh. We overcome the enemy by the Blood of the Lamb and by the word of our testimony and not loving our lives to the death. Our testimony is when we tell of God's redeeming grace in our lives. His grace is sufficient no matter the need or situation. I encourage you to continue to look to God. His grace is sufficient.

> Luke 9:16 *Then he took the five loaves and the two fishes,*
> *and looking up to heaven, he blessed them, and brake,*
> *and gave to the disciples to set before the multitude.*

# NOTES

# CHAPTER 6

# DELIVERANCE THROUGH CHRIST

# DELIVERANCE THROUGH CHRIST

**EXODUS 20:11** *For in six days the LORD made heaven and earth, the sea, and all that in them is, and rested the seventh day: wherefore the LORD blessed the sabbath day, and hallowed it.*

The number six prophetically symbolizes man and his human weakness. God created the earth and all of its contents in six days. On the seventh day God rested. God made man in His image on the sixth day thus six represents the number of man. I have been attending The School of the Prophets over the last several years at Cutting Edge Ministries. Our instructor Prophet Joe Brock shared an enlightening and to some a revolutionary teaching regarding the sixth day of Creation. Hebrews 4:8-11 read, "For if Jesus had given them rest, then would he not afterward have spoken of another day. There remaineth therefore a rest to the people of God. For he that is entered into his rest, he also hath ceased from his own works, as God did from his. Let us labour therefore to enter into that rest, lest any man fall after the same example of unbelief." Prophet Brock taught the group that once we accept Jesus as our Personal Savior we enter into His rest. Jesus is our Rest, our Peace and the Joy of our Salvation. Once we allow Him to renew our minds we gain the mind of Christ. He is ours and we are then His. On the contrary if you have not accepted Jesus as your Lord and Savior then you have not entered into His rest.

Prophet Brock explained that people ruled by the world's kingdom are still living in the sixth day. The born again, Blood bought redeemed of the Most High God have entered the seventh day through Christ. John 10:9 reads, "I am the door: by me if any man enter in, he shall be saved, and shall go in and out, and find pasture." Jesus is the door by which we enter into the rest of eternal life and rest in everyday life. He instructs us to cast our cares upon Him. We no longer strive to survive but learn to live to give. Through Him we overcome the rulers of this world and obtain life more abundantly. We receive His rest in *All through Christ: Christ through All.*

Revelation 13:16-18 reads, "And he causeth all, both small and great, rich and poor, free and bond, to receive a mark in their right hand, or in their foreheads: And that no man might buy sell, save he that had the mark, or the name of the beast, or the number of his name. Here is wisdom. Let him that hath understanding count the number of the beast: for it is the number of a man; and his number is Six hundred threescore and six." Prophet Brock explained that the prince of the air who is satan attempts to program the world's minds with his wicked agenda. Television and radio airwaves are used to promote the devil's evil plan. Prophet Joe Brock highlighted how people fear the future mark of the beast on their foreheads. He warns that the mark is already being placed upon the minds of worldly people. Primetime television is full of violence, reprobate sexual behavior and drugs. There is emphasis of the love of money and not the love of God.

I have been attending a course based on Bill and Michael French's book, *The Remedy,* for the last couple of years. The class and book discuss deliverance ministry and they both emphasize Jesus as the remedy to all of our ills. We meet monthly at Advocate Ministries in Irondale, Alabama. A point that was emphasized in the class and book is that you can't cast out the flesh. We can choose to crucify the flesh with its sinful desires or not. We are all given free will and are allowed to choose whether to live for God or not. We each have a daily choice whether or not to die to our carnal man. The Apostle Paul writes in I Corinthians 15:31, "I protest by your rejoicing which I have in Christ

Jesus our Lord, I die daily." We as believers in Christ choose whether or not to die daily. The Holy Spirit draws but it is still our choice to answer His call.

I labored in prayer day after day for a beloved family member. I sought the Lord on their behalf. I asked the Lord to speak to their heart like He mercifully had done to mine. On one such morning while crying out to my Savior I audibly heard, "I did, they chose." Life is choice driven you live or you die by the choices you make. God is the Good Shephard and He leads rather than drives. He draws and does not prod. The Holy Spirit is a gentleman. He draws us. He does not make us. James 4:7-8 reads, "Submit yourselves therefore to God. Resist the devil, and he will flee from you. Draw nigh to God, and he will draw nigh to you. Cleanse your hands, ye sinners; and purify your hearts, ye double minded."

The devil prods and drives with his arsenal of anger, assumption and accusation. The enemy of our soul is subtle and sinister. He operates under the camouflage of half -truths and insinuations. Witchcraft is often erroneously envisioned as a woman in a pointy black hat who is stirring a pot. The enemy does stir stuff up but he wears many different hats. He is often outfitted in a business suit and tie. He is a wolf in sheep's clothing. 1 Samuel 15:23 reads, "For rebellion is as the sin of witchcraft, and stubbornness is as iniquity and idolatry. Because thou hast rejected the word of the Lord, he hath also rejected thee from being king." This scripture speaks of the fall of King Saul but many people today unknowingly and sometimes knowingly allow this wicked force to work through them.

A person who intentionally plants a seed of distrust through innuendo is operating in witchcraft. An example is someone telling a young husband that they saw his wife kissing her "old boyfriend" yesterday. After much questioning and disruption of peace the bearer of half- truths points out that the newly-weds were ONCE boyfriend and girlfriend. The tongue wagger had only seen the happily married couple kissing each other. One of my husband's favorite saying is to not let the tail wag the dog. He also says, don't allow jealousy to "pillage the village." Misery loves company. A seed of jealousy and distrust can be planted through the guise of friendly ruse. Witchcraft is a spirit that the devil utilizes to attack and attempt to weaken a person's mind and fortitude. The spirit of witchcraft is evil, controlling and rebellious. It attempts to usurp rightful authority. It tries to dismantle God given and ordained power. This spirit wants to gain a foothold in your mind through manipulation. Scripture defines the enemy's goal as to steal, kill and destroy. He attempts to steal your peace. God in contrast wants us to be still and know that He is God. The enemy wants your joy and to destroy your reputation and morale. John 10:10 reads, "The thief cometh not, but for to steal, and to kill, and to destroy: I am come that they might have life, and that they might have it more abundantly."

The battlefield is in our minds. The land mines are often whispers of deception and deceit. I was counseling a young lady who was struggling with alien thoughts. They were attempting to diminish her self-worth. I advised her to practice screening her thought life. The filter to determine what to accept or reject should be based on the Word of God. We should define who we are and our self-worth by the Word's standards. We should not judge ourselves by the world's standards. In contrast what an ungodly man considers good or bad, acceptable or unacceptable often changes depending on who is around or not. Be not deceived God is not mocked and He changes not. The Bible is our manual on living. As Christians, Christ is our example and role model.

The Gospel describes an epileptic boy brought to Jesus's disciples by his father. The boy was in need of deliverance. The disciples were unable to cure the child. The desperate father beseeched the Great Physician to heal his sick and suffering son. Jesus cast the demon out of the boy. Our merciful Savior grabbed the lad's hands and lifted him up. All things are possible with God. Nothing is too hard for our God. When man fails you just look up. God is the lifter up of our heads.

Our Father is compassionate and hearkens to the cries of His children. Scripture says that He bottles every one of our tears. He even knows the number of hairs on our heads. Jesus reached down and picked the young epileptic boy up out of the dirt. Others had given up on him but Jesus lifted him up. Glory to God, Jesus will do the same today for me and you. Jesus is still the lifter up of our heads. Our Savior extended His arms for the world on Calvary. The boy's situation looked grim. Many of ours days look dark but we must see God's only Son as the Light in our darkness. Mark 9:23-24 reads, "Jesus said unto him, If thou canst believe, all things are possible to him that believeth. And straightway the father of the child cried out, and said with tears, Lord, I believe; help thou mine unbelief."

During His time on earth, Jesus healed and delivered many hurting people from demonic strongholds. Oddly though healing and deliverance ministries are no longer accepted and/or appreciated in many mainstream churches. God is still a Healer and a Deliverer. The Book of Malachi proclaims that He is the LORD GOD and He changes not. If Jesus healed people then, if He delivered them then I have faith that Jesus still heals and delivers today. I am not telling you what I think but what I know. I am a living testimony of God's Amazing Grace. He healed and delivered me. The song writer John Newton was a former slave trader. He summarizes the ministry of deliverance in the song he penned, "Amazing Grace". The man once known as "The Great Blasphemer" beautifully wrote these lovely lyrics. Newton proclaimed that "I once was lost but now am found, was blind, but now, I see." Newton remembered his day of redemption while journaling. He wrote, "On that day the Lord sent from on high and delivered me out of deep waters." John Newton's ministry was influential in Britain's abolition of slavery. Jesus came to set the captives free from whatever or whomever held them bound. Jesus is the Beginning and the End. Psalm 90:4 reads, "For a thousand years in thy sight are but as yesterday when it is past, and as a watch in the night."

We all have a story to tell but our tale should point others toward God. We should broadcast His faithfulness rather than be self-promoting or even self-demoting. We all have a past but now we have a future when we accept Christ. The key to living the abundant life in Christ is receiving your new beginning in Him. I have been blessed with the opportunity to provide medical and spiritual care for women as they escape the sex trade industry. Compassion and a kind word goes a long way in healing a hurting soul. Don't allow the regrets of your past to haunt your present or hinder your future. Jesus is our beginning and our ending. He is the author and finisher of our faith. He knew us before the world was framed. God knows our predispositions and our weaknesses. Allow Him to be the perfector of our faith. Our uniqueness may be perceived by others as a weakness but it is truly the link to our purpose. The person's or group of person's pain you vicariously feel the most is divinely linked to your purpose. In your uniqueness rests your purpose. I was criticized as a child for my laugh being too boisterous and for being animated. Hundreds of patients have said that my laugh and sense of humor has blessed their hearts. Scripture reminds us that laughter does a heart good like medicine. One reason that I can minister effectively to hurting people in difficult situations is that I do not take myself too seriously. I am transparent enough to make my embarrassing moments the brunt of a teaching moment or as an ice breaker. You might not have been exactly where another person is but you can still offer them a hand up. The only time to look down on any individual is when you are offering them a hand up.

I was counselling a young lady who had made stellar achievements in corporate America despite her background of disparity and despair. She was raised in an urban housing project that was riddled by crime and poverty. The now successful mother and wife beat the odds but she was considering walking away from her six figure career. She was frustrated that after each battle for economic and racial equality there seemed to be another. The glass ceiling was elusively moving higher and higher after she achieved each new level of success. I was led to share with this woman of African-American heritage I sensed that she had a breaker spirit. Scripture describes that we all have a role to play. Some plant while others water but God gets the increase. Her row seemed so hard to row because her assignment was to break the soil in preparation for another to plant. This hard edged, no-nonsense lady's calling was birthed in the pain of socioeconomic and racial divide. She had personally faced injustice so it was easier for her to sense another's struggle. I encouraged her that her voice was needed in her primarily male Caucasian field. Her real job was not what she was hired for but to provide a voice for the voiceless. For example, her co-workers did not understand her bold and defiant tone when they proposed a new dress code policy. The increase in locs and braids in employees spurred the discussion of possibly prohibiting Afrocentric hair-styles. These natural looks were deemed "distracting" in a HR meeting. The woman with the "breaker-spirit" was the only person of color in the meeting. She boldly asked, "How can something be distracting when it is how it grows out of their heads." She informed the group that the many straight hair styles that they have become accustomed to have been chemically processed. We must stand up for who we are and whose we are. Assimilation and accommodation are not always the answers. We are a peculiar people and a chosen generation. You matter and you have been placed where you are for a reason. Allow God to get the increase in your life.

I was recently at prayer meeting. I was putting in yet another prayer request regarding one of my many struggles in my vocation as a physician. One of the older intercessors wisely pointed out that the group should pray for my strength in the storm rather than for the storm to be moved. She recognized and pointed out to me that I was being placed again and again in dark places because my purpose was to bring The Light. Ephesians 5:13 reads, "But all things that are exposed are made manifest by the light, for whatever makes manifest is light." Stop asking of the Lord, "Why me?" We may think we are being punished but consider our current conundrum a privilege. It is a privilege to allow His light to shine through you. The term drum major for justice was used during the Civil Rights Movement for its leaders. A drum major traditionally leads and directs a band. His or her role is to coordinate and orchestrate by example. Our job as believers should be to lead people to Christ by our example. 2 Corinthians 3:2-3 reads, "Ye are our epistle written in our hearts, known and read of all men: Forasmuch as ye ae manifestly declared to be the epistle of Christ ministered by us, written not with ink, but with Spirit of the living God; not in tables of stone, but in fleshly tables of the heart." Our lives are an open book for all to see. It is the closest thing to the Bible many people will ever read. We are living epistles. We are to be living examples of not just godly living but of God's love and justice. A saying that many of us grew up hearing is, "Do as I say and not as I do." That is an example of hypocrisy in action. We should strive rather to be examples of the love of Christ in action. We are the hands and feet of Jesus. We are instructed to pray for His will on earth as it is in heaven .Often though we hinder His work intentionally or unintentionally through sins of commission or omission. Even though we don't understand something or someone that does not make them wrong.

We also arrogantly and erroneously attempt to put God in a box. We pray a prayer but we have in our mind how we want God to answer it. We pray for Him to fix the problem. We seek His help because we don't know how to help ourselves. We then dare to complain when the outcome is not just how we imagined. A longed for gift is still the same gift no matter the wrapping. God knows our beginning and our end. A day to us is a thousand to Him. We cannot fathom the wisdom of Our Heavenly Father but we dare complain. Scripture encourages us that all things work out for the good for those who love God and that are called according to His purpose. Most medicine tastes bad going down but the end result is sweet. We are God's children. Until people reach a point of maturity they often do not know what is good for them. A baby does not know that a stove is hot. It is our responsibility as good parents to make sure our children's environments are safe until they can make proper choices. It is the same way with us. We might want to play with fire. For example, a man or woman might be too hot to handle but we keep trying to handle them. They are hot like fire. Please heed my warning. A pretty wrapping does not ensure a good gift. I treat a lot of people who are "burning". The average Joe or Joann would not know until they have experienced the heat and end up in the health clinic.

Many people have exited your life stage left because of God's grace and mercy. We cry, fuss and cuss about why "he did me like that" but it was truly for our good. Luke 11:11-13 reads, "If a son shall ask bread of any of you that is a father, will he give him a stone? Or if he ask a fish, will he for a fish give him a serpent? Or if he shall ask an egg, will he offer him a scorpion? If ye then, being evil, know how to give good gifts unto your children: how much more shall your heavenly Father give the Holy Spirit to them that ask him?" Snakes slither in close trying to go undetected until they are close enough to strike. Snakes shed their skin. They have an outer covering that is removed when they no longer have use for it. Deceitful people masquerade as whatever allows them intimate contact to their target. Eventually snakes shed their skin but by then it is often too late. Often times you have already gotten snake bit, by then. Two of my spiritual mentors described situations when they were talking to people and the Lord revealed to them what was beneath the surface. Both ladies saw the masks stripped before their eyes. They reported that the face of a serpent replaced the face of the person as they were conversing with them. Both of the prayer warriors were startled but finished conducting their business. This revelation did change how they handled the vipers that walked on two legs. One adder was in a church setting the other worked in a hospital. Eve was deceived by a snake in the Garden of Eden. There are still snakes among us today. I thank the Lord for giving us spiritual eyes to see, protect and direct. Scripture describes satan masquerading as an angel of light. One function of the

Holy Spirit is to warn us but it is our responsibility to heed the warning. We often ignore His still small voice. Warning precedes destruction.

Not by coincidence but by holy design while writing this portion of the book, my daughter came running in my room. She announced, "Daddy just killed a snake." My husband heard our dog barking vehemently so he went to the window to investigate. Our German Shephard was staring intently at what seemed to be the ground from my husband's vantage point from inside the house. My spouse then saw the head of a snake rise up above the thick grass. He immediately ran out of the back door all the while looking for a weapon to protect our family pet. Without the thought of self-preservation my husband jumped between the dog and their foe. He slayed the slithering serpent with a garden hoe. Our pet German Shepherd was later seen resting peacefully in the same grass. He fell asleep in the spot the intruder had earlier trespassed. Psalm 23:1-2 reads, "The LORD is my shepherd; I shall not want. He maketh me to lie down in green pastures: he leadeth me beside the still waters." We are to rest wholeheartedly in Our Heavenly Father's arms of protection. Be thankful rather than fearful when God reveals the snakes living among us. David was not afraid. The boy ran toward the giant Goliath and slew him with a stone. David chopped Goliath's head off and hoisted it into the air after he slayed him. There is no need to fear. God is with us, too. Scripture explains that the enemy does come in like a flood but the Spirit of the Lord lifts up a standard against him. Rest in God's peace, provision and power. He is a good, good Father. He would never give us a snake for a fish. Walk in God's power.

The day prior to the snake in our dog pen incident, I was led to walk the perimeter of our property and pray. I lingered as I prayed in the Spirit at the location the serpent appeared less than 24 hours later. Psalm 91:13 reads, "Thou shalt tread upon the lion and adder: the young lion and the dragon shalt thou trample under feet." The Holy Spirit warns but it is up to us to listen. During this period of time I had been in deep intercession for my family, job and church. I discerned a Spirit of Haman at work. Scripture tells us that we have the power in the name of Jesus to bind anything not of God's will. We can release His will on earth as it is in heaven. I Corinthians 12 continues to explain how the Holy Spirit disperses diverse gifts to God's people. I have been enrolled in a course with Advocate Ministries for the last couple of years. It is as discussed previously appropriately called The Remedy. The class details the utilization and usefulness of Deliverance Ministry in the Body of Christ for today. I Corinthians 12:10 reads, "To another the working of miracles; to another prophecy; to another discerning of spirits; to another divers kinds of tongues; to another the interpretation of tongues."

Haman was one of king Ahasuerus's key advisors. He plotted against God's people but his evil ploy was exposed and overturned. The Book of Esther tells how Haman sought to have all of the Jews killed by manipulating King Ahasuerus. Haman wanted the king to sign unjust edicts. Both Haman and the king were unaware that the new, beautiful queen was a Jew. God had a ram in the bush for Abraham and He had a Jewish girl named Esther in the palace for His people. Esther was in God's will and timing for a time such as this. Esther 4:14 reads, "For if thou altogether holdest thy peace at this time, then shall there enlargement and deliverance arise to the Jews from another place; but thou and thy father's house shall be destroyed: and who knoweth whether thou art come to the kingdom for such a time as this?" The gallows that Haman hung from were the same gallows he built for the Jews. Once Haman's deceit was discovered he was the one that dangled. Psalm 7:15 reads, "He made a pit, and digged it, and is fallen into the ditch which he made." Haman's gallows reminds me of the 1930's song, "Strange Fruit". The first verse says, "Southern trees bear strange fruit, Blood on the leaves and blood at the root, Black bodies swinging in the southern breeze, Strange fruit hanging from poplar trees." A People who do not know their history are doomed to repeat the mistakes of their past.

Sandra Bland, a Black Lives Matter supporter, was arrested and beaten after a routine traffic stop. Hours later she was found dead hanging from a garbage bag in her Texas jail cell. "Southern trees bear strange fruit". As a physician I have sat in on autopsies and have pronounced many people dead over the years as part of my on-call medical duties. In my medical expertise Sandra Bland's unaltered mug shot resembled a post-mortem picture. There was not a warrant out for her arrest. Sandra Bland was not one of America's Most Wanted. She was not wanted Dead or Alive. She only wanted to get to her new job at her alma mater.

I was sharing with my mentor, Pastor Beverly Jackson about some of the disrespectful treatment I was experiencing sadly still in the 21st century. As a black female in the traditionally white male dominated profession of medicine people attempt to call me by my first name. I have been addressed as the nurse even though introduced and understood to be the attending physician. Other female physicians and I have experienced nurses refusing to follow our patient care directives. This insubordination and disrespect is essentially unheard of with white male physicians. Pastor Jackson identified and prayed against a spirit of oppression that was attempting to rear its ugly head. Psalm 146:7 reads, "Which excecuteth judgment for the oppressed: which giveth food to the hungry. The LORD looseth the prisoners:" God is a deliverer no matter who the oppressor or oppressed are shown to be. God is a just god and justice shall prevail.

I had a dream during a difficult time in my life. There was a large light brown wolf wandering around me. The oddest thing about the dream was that I was not afraid of the beast. The animal had certain physical characteristics and mannerisms of one of my medical assistants. The Lord was warning me of a wolf in sheep's clothing. The dream pulled the covering off of the deceit that was right under my nose. Don't be fearful but be faithful.

Our God is a god against oppression of any kind. He sent His Only Begotten Son to set the captives free. He raised up Moses from a family of slaves to Pharaoh's house. Moses led the Children of Israel through the wilderness. He raised up Harriet Tubman from a slave to become the "Black Moses". She was the conductor of the Underground Railroad. Black Moses led thousands of slaves, of African descent through the woods of the South, to a place of Northern freedom. God still leads and directs but we have to listen to His still small voice. I was amazed by the organization and ingenuity of the Underground Railroad. I was given the opportunity to retrace some of its stops and the escaped slave's steps. I saw the nickel sized openings in the floor boards of a Southern church which served as their air holes. I saw the quilts that not only covered my ancestor's cold brown shoulders but served as a pictorial map to direct their paths. The children of Israel was given a cloud by day and a pillar of fire by night to direct them through their wilderness. A wilderness is still a wilderness today. Slavery by another name is still slavery today. Oppression was oppression then and it is still oppression now. There is a near eighty percent pay gap difference between men and women in the United States' workforce. Exodus 22:21 reminds us, "Thou shalt neither vex a stranger, nor oppress him: for ye were strangers in the land of Egypt."

A caller from Texas on my radio show, "What up Doc?" called for prayer regarding his ministry. As we prayed I sensed a python spirit. I cautioned this young man that this evil but seductive spirit was trying to squeeze the very life out of him. The spirit of a serpent was trying to oppress him. The enemy's plan was to steal his energy and passion so he would give up in frustration. John 10:10 reads, "The thief cometh not, but to steal, and to kill, and to destroy: I am come that they might have life, and that they might have it more abundantly." I spoke life over this minister of the Gospel of Jesus Christ. I pled the Blood of Jesus over him and his calling. The devil's plot had to cease and desist. The Blood still works. The call ended with a sense of invigoration and renewal of purpose from the caller. He had regained his peace and his faith was strengthened. I encourage you today not to give up. Get up and keep pressing forward toward the mark in Jesus name. Forward march.

I was led to blow slow gentle bursts of air into the microphone as I prayed for the caller. The Greek word pneuma means spirit or wind. The Book of Genesis depicts God breathing His Spirit, The Breath of Life into Adam. As a prophetic intercessor I am often led in faith to make certain symbolic actions during prayer. We walk by faith and not by sight. No matter how a thing might look to another person, I have learned to walk by faith and not by sight. Many times I don't even understand the spiritual significance of my actions. The wind blows whichever way it chooses. God can choose to deliver any way that He so desires. I just thank the Lord for His deliverance. John 3:8 reads, "The wind bloweth where it listeth, and thou hearest the sound thereof, but canst not tell whence it cometh, and whither it goeth: so is every one that is born of the Spirit."

Oftentimes the instructions will not make sense to us naturally. God's ways are above our ways. He is a spirit and will communicate with us Spirit to spirit. This form of communication bypasses the soulish realm which includes our human intellect and emotions. I was once driving to a colleague's open house for her new medical practice. I felt the unction to take a different route. It did not make common sense to go the long way on side roads. I could just take the interstate. I did not listen to the prompting of the Spirit and I was rear-ended by a distracted driver. The long way was God's way of leading me in a safe path. Ironically, my "shortcut" took me hours longer and added much aggravation and expense. I recently was given the opportunity to speak at a women's group. My topic was on discovering and developing our talents. I emphasized to the ladies to not only stay in God's will but also in His timing. Warning comes before destruction but it is up to us to heed the warning. The Spirit leads, encourages, prompts and gives direction but He does not force. We have free-will to follow His lead or not.

It is our choice whether we submit to the fact that His strength is made perfect in our weaknesses. We submit by surrendering our will to His. I was given a vision years ago which I share with patients and in my book *Fountain in the Valley*. It visually depicted the peace of godly surrender. On one specific occasion, I was given the opportunity to minister to a young woman. The lady was seeing a psychiatrist for anxiety. She'd been taught deep breathing relaxation techniques but she was still struggling with panic attacks. I was led to describe the vision the Lord gave that helped calm my fears. The wife and mother was experiencing anxiety. She was trying to figure out her purpose in her changing family dynamics. Her role as caregiver was brought into question as her children became young adults. Who was she as her life transitioned? We should never forget that we are God's and He is ours. Seasons may change but His love, the Lover of Our Soul will not. I had to learn through tumultuous trials that my identity was not in my titles, achievements or degrees. I am a child of God and most importantly He is my Father.

Once we comprehend that nothing can separate His love from us we then find His peace. He will never leave us nor forsake us. We only have to relax and receive His love and grace. In the vision I was tranquilly floating in the warm, Gulf of Mexico waters. The waves were crashing one after the other. I remained above water as long as I kept looking up and stayed relaxed. In the vision whenever I began to struggle or fight the water I would immediately begin to sink. Relax and keep your eyes focused on the Lord and Savior even when the waves of life crash down. He is the Lifter of Your Head. He is your Help. He is your Strength. You only have to look up. Peter walked on water until he took his eyes off Jesus. You can rise to any occasion and overcome any opposition with The Maker of Heaven of Earth on your side.

I told the distraught mother and wife about this difficult period of time in my life. I was in a physically, emotionally and financially strained situation. I had prayed about the obstacles but I kept trying to use earthly contacts and connections to move them. Instead of being still and learning the lesson from the testing, I kept fighting the process. Psalm 46:10 reads, "Be still, and know that I am God: I will be exalted among the heathen, I will be exalted in the earth." As I look back, I can see with the 20/20 vision what only hindsight provides. I was in a season of purification. There were some things in me and some people around me that the Lord wanted to remove. He knew that I had a journey ahead of me and I needed to pack lightly. Old habits, rotten relationships and antiquated mindsets were holding me back from the best my Father had in store. I could not float because I was carrying too much baggage. God was readying me for a new season. He had to remove the old to make room for the new. Isaiah 43:19 reads, "Behold, I will do a new thing; now it shall spring forth; shall ye not know it? I will even make a way in the wilderness, and rivers in the desert." God was trying to do a new thing in my life but I was holding on to the old. I encourage you to Let Go and Let God. Let go of pride, past mistakes, resentment and retaliation. Allow God to fight your battles and keep your peace.

As a child I watched professional wrestling on television and became familiar with the term submission move. Often times we need a wakeup call. Ephesians 5:14 reads, "Wherefore he saith, Awake thou that sleepest, and arise from the dead, and Christ shall give thee light." This awakening allows us to realize our own human weakness and dependence on God. Jacob experienced a life changing, limp inflicting submission move when he attempted to wrestle with an angel. Jacob cunned his brother out of his birthright but God still had a plan for Jacob. To be used by God, Jacob needed to submit to God's way. He had to abandon his wayward path. A common colloquial saying is that our arms are too short to box with God. God desires that we give Him our failures and faults and allow Him to refine us as pure gold. Oftentimes the furnace of affliction is needed to direct our desires toward God. Isaiah 48:9-11 reads, "For my name's sake will I defer mine anger, and for my praise will I refrain for thee, that I cut thee not off. Behold, I have refined thee, but not with silver; I have chosen thee in the furnace of affliction. For mine own sake, even for mine own sake, will I do it: for how should my name be polluted? and I will not give my glory unto another."

Jesus wants to be Our Lord and Savior. He alone is the Savior of the world. Pride comes before a fall. A fall from grace is many times preempted by us trying to steal God's glory. God graciously saves, heals, delivers or protects us. We then have the audacity to hand over the accolades to a mere person. We give His glory to a person that God placed in our path to help us. God deserves all the glory, honor and praise. I am nothing without Him. I can't breathe, think, let alone function as a physician without God. He is my All and All and I know that I am nothing without Him. Knowing that His strength is made perfect in our weakness is empowering. You don't have to do it on your own. Give it to God.

We were preparing for a weekend retreat to minister to teenagers. One of the spiritual leaders told the group his testimony. He candidly said that he worked hard to provide for his family. He tried to be a godly husband and father. He experienced burn out because he was attempting to do it all in his strength. People often misinterpret the term fleshly as only fulfilling immoral desires. But, we as Christians can get in the flesh when we try to do God's will in our own strength, power and intellect. This big, burly man confided to and encouraged this group of mostly women. He revealed that he was truly free and strong only when he recognized his weakness and dependence on God. John 3:6 reads, "That which is born of the flesh is flesh; and that which is born of the Spirit is spirit." *All Through Christ: Christ Through All.* We should receive our deliverance through Christ.

I did not personally come to realize my dependence on my Heavenly Father on a soft bed of roses. I had to feel some thorns. The pain woke me up to my own mortality and weaknesses. My grandmother used to say that a hard head makes a soft tail. This is an example of mother wit. It means that if you are so hard-headed or rebellious that a lesson can't be taught by words or from seeing another's experiences then you might go through painful situations. These uncomfortable circumstances can often be avoided by obedience. King Saul learned the lesson that obedience is better than sacrifice. He refused to obey God's instructions on how to defeat the Amekelites. Saul kept the best sheep, oxen and lambs rather than following the specific directions from the priest. Samuel the priest clearly told Saul to destroy them ALL. Saul sheepishly explained that he planned on sacrificing the animals to God that he kept in reserve. Obedience is better than sacrifice. Saul eventually lost his mind, reputation and kingdom.

God knows what is best for us. He is all knowing. He is the Ancient of Days. He knows our beginning and our end. Pride and arrogance can hijack God's best for our lives. Humility and submission to godly authority have been my saving grace on more than one occasion. I have had the opportunity to assist in training many health care professionals. The most dangerous personality flaw in a doctor or nurse is an arrogant and unteachable spirit. Lives can be lost if you overestimate your abilities and are unwilling to ask for assistance. In the ministry souls can be lost if we overestimate our own natural abilities. No matter how big our ministries have become we should never stop leaning and depending on God. His grace is sufficient and obedience is better than sacrifice. We might have preached hundreds of sermons but we should still listen for His still small voice before we speak to His people. Callings can become clouded and lives can be made complicated when we start listening for the applause of man more than the Holy Spirit. The quantity of amens and accolades do not measure the quality of a sermon but the obedience to the Spirit does. I was listening to a local television evangelist while getting ready for church this morning. She said that we can find a church, if we look hard enough that will justify and accept any sin we would like to commit. Right is right and wrong is wrong. The people of God should not sugar coat the gospel. We are not seeking man's approval but the approval of Our Heavenly Father. 2 Timothy 4:3 reads, "For the time will come when they will not endure sound doctrine; but after their own lusts shall they heap to themselves teachers, having itching ears;"

The parable of the talents in Mathew likens the kingdom of heaven to a man who is going away on a trip. He leaves three of his servants varying amounts of talents to take care of in his absence. Two of them double the amount given before the master returns. They were told, "Well done my good and faithful servants." The person who hid his talent and did not produce a productive return was called slothful and wicked. You know a tree by the type of fruit it produces. Many people claim to be of God but what does their fruit demonstrate. The fruit of the Spirit is love, joy, peace, longsuffering, gentles, goodness, faith, meekness and self- control. God's people have His spirit living within them and display His fruit on the outside of them. A child of God shows His Father's fruit on Sunday morning and on Monday through Friday. They show love to all people not just the ones that look or sound like them. Love is what love does. You can say you love someone but as the 80's pop song says, "What have you done for me lately." Many believers erroneously view their relationship with God through this skewed catch phrase. They temper their service to the Lord by what they perceive He has done for them lately. God is good all the time. He is good in the bad times and in the good times. Our faith is developed in valley seasons. We should stop complaining and start trusting our faithful God. He is working it out for our good. The test will become a testimony, if we do not lose confidence. Hebrew 10:35 reads, "Cast not away therefore your confidence, which hath great recompense of reward." God is the rewarder of those who diligently seek Him. Seek

Him and not worldly riches that rust, fade and wither. Benny Hinn writes in his book, *Anointing,* "He longs for us to know and experience His presence and His anointing. When we are emptied of self, we will know His presence. Only then can we experience His power—the anointing of the Holy Spirit. But the trust factor is also very important. We must be faithful with what God so richly supplies."

I knew the following story needed to be told. I struggled with fear of man so it did not make it into my last book. While I was editing my rough draft of *Fountain in the Valley* I had a very disturbing experience. The Lord gave me confirmation today that now was the time to share the details of this disturbing event which occurred over a year ago. My confirmation came while attending my monthly class on deliverance at Advocate Ministries. Prophet Joe Brock closed the conference with an account of a spiritual attack that he recently overcame. He recapped the story that occurred the previous Sunday. His telephone App alarmed because the security camera in his home detected motion. No one was at home. He and his family were at church and Prophet Brock was about to start ministering. His eldest son opened the cell phone pictures to determine the disturbance in the home. From the expression on his son's face, Prophet Brock knew he needed to see what was happening at his house. He viewed the images and saw an at least 8 foot tall spirit cloaked in black hovering in his den. He showed the pictures to the church congregation. They said it looked like the, "grim reaper". The church began to pray. After prayer, within a few frames a blue light came and engulfed the trespasser. Light overcomes darkness and the prayers of the righteous avails much.

Scripture explains that we struggle not against flesh and blood. It is against principalities, powers, rulers of darkness of this world and against spiritual wickedness in high places. But, Glory to God at the name of Jesus every knee shall bow and ever tongue shall confess that Jesus Christ is Lord. Ephesians 1:20-22 reads, "Which he wrought in Christ, when he raised him from the dead, and set him at his own right hand in the heavenly places, Far above all principality, and power, and might, and dominion, and every name that is named, not only in this world, but also in that is to come: And hath put all things under his feet, and gave him to be the head over all things to the church,". Prophet Brock had recently taken on a new ministerial role in Advocate Ministries. The enemy was trying to intimidate and instill fear in his children to reach him. The enemy failed. His story strengthened many including me. He encouraged my faith enough to share my story.

Perfect love casts out fear and Jesus is perfect love. He came to set the captives free from whatever has them bound. Fear has torment but Jesus is perfect love and peace. Similarly my story of God's deliverance occurred after an evil intruder attempted to intimidate and instill fear. God's Holy Word says in Colossians 1:13 reads, "Who hath delivered us from the power of darkness, and hath translated us into the kingdom of his dear Son:" We have been bought with a price and our redeemer lives. No matter what comes up against us whether it is natural or supernatural it has to bow at the name of Jesus. A year or so ago I was on a Christian retreat with my daughter. We were having a wonderful time. We were sharing in godly fellowship. We were developing our relationship with God and with each other. Each day was filled with educational tours, dramas and viewing Christian artifacts. Once we returned to our room, the nights were just as inspirational and enlightening. Our roommate was a strong believer and she is a pastor's wife. We would sing and discuss scriptures into the night. In addition I was finishing the editing process of *Fountain in the Valley*. I was enthralled this particular evening because my teenage daughter was engaged in the Bible discussion. She even boldly offered some prophetic words. Acts 2:17 reads, "And it shall come to pass in the last days, saith God, I will pour out of my Spirit upon all flesh: and your sons and your daughters shall prophesy, and your young men shall see visions, and your old men shall dream dreams;" The atmosphere in the room was anointed and bathed in prayer and praise. So, to our surprise and dismay we were all awakened around 1:00 am with an evil, eerie presence in the hotel room. It was pitch black in the room but there was an ominous being hovering over the double bed that I was sharing with my daughter. I remember asking, "Who are you?" I heard in a disturbingly demonic voice, "It is I." My child, my only daughter was screaming in terror as the spirit tried to lift her from the bed. I tried to come between my daughter and the demonic force. The haze of chaos was so thick in the room. When I tried to pray, the fog of confusion in the room clouded my mind. The evilness was so permeating that I could barely form sentences. I struggled to utter a prayer. I could barely cry out, "Jesus, Jesus, Jesus". I dropped to my knees at the edge of the bed in prayer. Our roommate turned the light on in the darkened room. She found me with a bloodied, busted lip. My daughter had huge hand prints singed onto both of her wrists. We all prayed and comforted each other and alerted the intercessors on the trip to pray. It was a spiritual attack sent to intimidate us. The enemy wanted to scare us enough not to continue seeking the things of God. God is faithful and at the name of Jesus every knee shall bow. As we screamed the name of Jesus, the Great I Am came and saved His children. The battle is the Lords. No matter how much we love our children, He loves them more.

I dedicated my children back to God when they were infants. I learned that night that Our Father is faithful to defend and care for us. I know my God is a strong tower. I cried out to Him and He came and rescued us. Proverbs 18:10 reads, "The name of the LORD is a strong tower: the righteous runneth into it, and is safe." I would be lying if I said I was not afraid. I was terrified but God's strength is made perfect in our weakness. I encourage you in whatever you are facing to trust God. I was literally beat up because I stepped into a spiritual battle fighting with my natural might. I acknowledged that it was not my battle when I dropped to my knees in submission. The battle is and was the Lords. We should move back and allow Him to fight on our behalf. Jesus is Our Defender and Our Protector. The Holy Spirit is

Our Comforter and Our Help. Often times we just need to step back and let Our Help, help.

You have to totally relax to float. You can't fight the water and expect to survive. You can't fight the process and thrive. God is with us and He promises to fight our battles. Our role often is to be still and know that He is God. The book *Needless Casualties of War* by John Paul Jackson taught me many great lessons on spiritual warfare. There are rules of engagement that we must be aware of in order to strategically defeat the enemy of our souls. He writes, "We do this as a kingdom of priests, embracing a spirit of worship directed toward God. Worship is foundational to advancing the Kingdom of God. It is giving focused attention to God, and requires that we fix our eyes on Jesus (Hebrews 12:2). It is Satan who desires to steal our attention away from Jesus. Frankly, my determined focus is to seek first the Kingdom of God and His righteousness, humble myself, and pray." There is deliverance through Christ.

Submission is one of the hardest lessons in this self-sufficient world. We value independence rather than interdependence. Worship of God is a stance of submission to His omnipotence. We should never forget regardless of our circumstances that He is all powerful. Ironically two of the common positions of worship: laying prostate before Him and lifting up holy hands are physically compromising positions. You can't rationally defend yourself from a threat bowed down with your head hanging low or with your hands raised in the air. Boxers are trained to protect their heads in a match. We as believers do not wrestle against flesh and blood. Our position of authority, power, strength and safety is only in submission to Our Heavenly Father. He will place us in the cleft of The Rock and in the shelter of His wings. All through Christ and Christ through all. The spirit intruder left the room after I knelt in submission to God's authority. I got caught in the cross-fire as long as I tried to fight a spiritual battle with physical tactics.

Scripture reminds us that the foolishness of God is wiser than man. One of the Foot Soldiers in the Civil Rights Movement told me how Dr. Martin Luther King directed them to kneel and pray. They were facing one of Bull Conner's assaults in Birmingham, Alabama. The position of kneeling before God to the carnal eye seemed a position of physical weakness. This posture ensured physical and spiritual success. I Corinthians 15:46 reads, "Howbeit that was not first which is spiritual, but that which is natural, and afterward that which is spiritual." God kept them then and He is still a Keeper today. Civil unrest was sparked again in 2014 when Michael Brown a black young man was shot and killed by a white Ferguson, Missouri police officer. Many protestors showed their support and solidarity by raising their arms on football fields and basketball courts. This 18 year-old African-American was unarmed. He had no weapon.

Spiritually, I would like to remind you that no weapon formed against us shall prosper as long as we are submitted to Our God. Scripture says that this is the heritage of the servants of the Lord for our righteousness is from Him. When we are not submitted to God and our minds are not renewed then His ways are not our ways. A people who does not know its history is doomed to repeat its mistakes. I strive to live by the African proverb, "Once you learn, you teach". Once you learn that we are all created equally and that God is no respect of persons then you live likewise. Each one teach one. Each one live to show God's love. God is love and perfect love is Jesus. He casts out all fear. Fear has torment and is the root of prejudices and hate. We must examine ourselves and our actions to determine if we are living in love or walking in fear. Wisdom is discerning the difference and determining distinguishing characteristics. Proverbs tells us that wisdom is the principal thing and with all our getting to get understanding. Ignorance is not bliss but knowledge is power. Not knowing is not an excuse. It can be dangerous to you and yours. Scripture reminds us that people perish for the lack of knowledge. I have noticed during my medical career and through the training and supervising of medical professionals that pride truly comes before a fall. Students and people in general who overestimate their abilities are dangerous to themselves and others. I have heard of horrible mishaps in the operating room because of a surgeon's cockiness and conceit. We should acknowledge our limitations and depend on our God's strength. Oftentimes we try to work in our own power and strength rather than charging up with His dunamis power.

A sex scandal rocked a minister's television ministry. The pastor was accused of having illicit affairs with young men in his congregation. The news was disturbing on so many levels. The betrayal of trust between a person of the cloth and his parishioners socked many in the gut. This was a subject of discussion and counseling with many of my male patients for several months. It hit many guys on a visceral level. A young man who accused the popular evangelist tearfully said he could not forget the scent of his pastor's cologne.

The amygdala are portions of our brain that help us integrate emotions. It receives emotions from our senses. Our five senses are hearing, sight, touch, smell and taste. A smell especially can trigger strong emotional responses. My grandmother died a decade ago. I smelled someone wearing my granny's preferred perfume in recent years. The aroma still transported me back to my youth. Regarding the sex scandal, one gentleman said that hearing that the boy could not get the accused pastor's scent out of his mind especially hurt him. It reminded the man of his relationship with his godly grandfather. As a child his granddad would help him tie his tie. He still lovingly remembers the scent of his grandfather's cologne half-a-century ago. Pleasant memories or events from a painful past can be unearthed by the sense of smell. We can't bury our past hurts. Hurting people hurt people. Many abusers were once abused. Seek God and Seek help. Things that are buried and not dealt with will sprout up in another season.

Praise confuses the enemy and the prayers of the righteous avails much. When God speaks a word of wisdom on how to defeat your foes or accomplish your goals don't try to figure it out. Just walk it out. We walk by faith and not by sight. Goliath fell from a stone hurled from David's sling shot. The future king encouraged himself in the Lord with these words of remembrance. He recounted the victories over the bear and lion that God gave Him and proclaimed the victory over Goliath. At the name of Jesus every knee shall bow no matter how big or how long it has loomed over us. God gave Joshua a word on how to defeat their enemy and the walls of Jericho came tumbling down. Joshua 6:16 reads, "And it came to pass at the seventh time, when the priests blew with the trumpets, Joshua said unto the people, Shout; for the Lord hath given you the city." Praise confuses the enemy and God inhabits the praises of His people. We walk by faith and not by sight.

We should strive not just for riches that corrode and fade but seek the wisdom of God. Seek Him and you shall find Him. Knock and the door shall be opened unto you. I shared a word of wisdom and knowledge with a young lady recently. I literally heard "knocking" in the spirit. I discerned that the Lord had been trying to get her attention. I shared a vitally important message that was laid upon my heart. We met paths months later and she tearfully yet joyfully said that her life was preserved from a hidden health danger. The enemy comes to steal, kill and destroy. Jesus, who is the Word of God made flesh has come to give us life and life more abundantly.

Many of us have taken licks from the enemy because we took natural weapons into a spiritual battle. 2 Corinthians 10:3 reads, "For though we walk in the flesh, we do not war after the flesh: (For the weapons of our warfare are not carnal, but mighty through God to the pulling down of strong holds ;)". The evil spirit in the hotel room identified itself as, "It is I". The devil is an imitator and an intimidator. When God instructed Moses on His plan of deliverance for the Children of Israel He told Moses to tell Pharaoh that "I AM" had sent him. Our God is the Only One and True and Living God. He is the Great I AM. Our God is all that we need. Jesus is the King of kings and the Lord of lords. He has already won the battle on our behalf. The enemy of our soul was defeated by the lover of our soul when He rose so long ago. He rose so we can stand in faith and in His strength. Jesus died on a cross on Golgotha's hill but three days later the tomb was found empty. Jesus conquered death, hell and the grave. Through Him we walk in victory. *All through Christ: Christ through All.* We have deliverance through Christ. Our God is all powerful. He is the maker of heaven and earth.

**EXODUS 20:11** *For in six days the LORD made heaven and earth, the sea, and all that is, and rested the seventh day: wherefore the LORD blessed the sabbath day, and hallowed it.*

# NOTES

# CHAPTER 7

# COMPLETENESS THROUGH CHRIST

# COMPLETENESS THROUGH CHRIST

**Joshua 6:4** *And seven priests shall bear before the ark seven trumpets of rams' horns: and the seventh day ye shall compass the city seven times, and the priests shall blow with the trumpets.*

The number seven prophetically symbolizes God's completeness, perfection and wholeness. Joshua followed God's instructions precisely. After the seventh turn around the wall there was a turn of events. The walls of Jericho came down. Through our God's power and grace the walls that fenced us in will also fall. I wrote the first few sentences of Chapter 7 before church. Pastor David Weir at Victory Church began a series on God's seven promises to Abraham that morning. In his introduction he said that the number seven symbolizes completeness. I thank God for confirmation that I was on the right track in this book. Sometimes we feel inadequate for a task. Our completeness is not in what we know but in who we know. Our completeness is in Christ. We don't have to know all the answers or pretend that we do. We pray and seek guidance from the One who wrote the Book. Presumption and assumption are dangerous. We should allow God to take the lead. We will then always end up in the right place in His perfect timing.

Genesis the 17th chapter chronicles the seven promises of life and blessings that God bestowed upon Abraham and his seed. Glory to God that we are the sons and daughters of Abraham engrafted into God's family by the Blood of Jesus. Galatians 3:7 reminds us, "Know ye therefore that they which are of faith, the same are the children of

Abraham." El Shaddai the all-powerful, omnipotent, only true and living God loves and cares for His children. He cares for us and takes care of us. He owns the cattle on a thousand hills. We have to be ever so careful to not worship the provision or the blessings. We should keep our eyes on The Provider and Blesser and stop focusing on the provision. Abraham's faith was challenged when He was asked to sacrifice the son of the promise. Benny Hinn warns in his book, *Anointing,* "He must deal with the idols and the sins in your heart. Any Isaacs in your heart must die (which is what God was determining with Abraham)".

He is the God that healeth us. Jesus healed the ten lepers but only one returned to give thanks. The Son of God proclaimed that this Samaritan who showed gratitude was not just healed but was made whole. Our wholeness, our completeness is only found in our relationship with the perfect one Christ. We are triune beings, body, soul and spirit. Our spirit is composed of our will mind and emotions. I see people on a daily basis who are hurting physically but the root cause is from an emotional wound or a spiritual void. I often hear broken people looking for wholeness, happiness and completeness in another person. Many times they seek medical care for depression, anxiety, addiction and psychosomatic complaints. The real problem is a spiritual void that can only be filled with a personal relationship with Jesus Christ.

We were created to worship God. We were created to be in relationship with our Heavenly Father. Our soul longs for an intimate interaction with Our Creator. Psalm 42:1 describes how like the deer pants for streams of water, so our soul pants for Our God. Jesus is the Living Water. Once you allow Him into your heart you will never thirst again. Benny Hinn explains in *Anointing,* "And that is exactly what happens to us. Our soul thirsts to come before the living God; it thirsts for His presence. David's imagery is perfect. A deer seeks water for two reasons; one, because he is thirsty and, two, because he is being chased by another animal. He knows that his scent will be lost if he gets into the water. He will be safe. So it is with us believers. We thirst for the presence of God because it satisfies our souls and because no enemy can touch us." We are whole in Christ. We have a hole in our soul without Him.

As a physician, I have treated many people at the end of life. I have been told that one of the most uncomfortable feelings is extreme thirst and a parched mouth. Even if they are unable to tolerate drinking liquids we compassionately dampen their mouths with a sponge of water. The Son of God while hanging on the cross for the sins of the world said, "I thirst". His accusers showed no compassion. They spitefully filled a sponge with vinegar rather than giving a dying man a drink of water. Matthew 5:44 reads, "But I say unto you, Love your enemies, bless them that curse you, do good to them that hate you, and pray for them which despitefully use you, and persecute you." Jesus is our example on living and forgiving. He prayed for the soldiers' souls while yet on the cross. Jesus asked Our Heavenly Father to forgive them for they knew not what they did. I have found during the bitter times of my life that once I reached the point of praying for my enemies that things became remarkably better. Strive to become better and not bitter through your trials. Prayer not only changed the situation but also my heart. Scriptures reminds us that out of the heart flow the issues of life. If we submit our hurts and pains to the Lord in prayer He can then heal our broken hearts. I have faced my share of lies and deceit. I have learned that unforgiveness and seeking revenge hurts you more than the other person. Allow God to fight your battles and receive His peace that surpasses all understanding.

I was bitter that I had to leave my practice of ten years because of unscrupulous people doing illegal things. I was even more frustrated that I followed the policy and procedure of reporting wrongdoing without avail. I left for a peace of mind and for my safety. The more I kept looking back the more bitter I became. The Lord reminded me of the story of the children of Israel and how they complained on their way to the Promised Land. God provided for them and He still provides for us today. My Pastor, Dr. David Craig often says that we are complaining with a loaf of bread under each arm. The children of Israel complained with manna or bread from heaven falling to meet their physical needs. We have the Bread of Life who is Jesus.

God expanded my territory and area of influence. 1 Chronicles 4:10 reads, "And Jabez called on the God of Israel, saying, Oh that thou wouldest bless me indeed, and enlarge my coast, and that thine hand might be with me, and that thou wouldest keep me from evil, that if may not grieve me! And God granted him that which he requested." Within my first month in my new practice location God allowed me to diagnose two cases of previously missed cancer. Both patients returned with tears of joy thanking me for allowing the Lord to work through me. Glory to God for things He has done and is doing.

Lot's wife turned into a pillar of salt when she longingly looked back at Sodom and Gomorrah. We too, can become stagnated by looking back rather than forward. We are to press toward the mark of the high calling of God in Christ Jesus. We are to put our hands to the plow and push. Luke 9:62 reads, "And Jesus said unto him, No man, having put his hand to the plough, and looking back, is fit for the kingdom of God."

How bitter that vinegar soaked sponge would have tasted to Jesus but He still compassionately removed the bitter sting from death. In the natural, a human can survive on average a week without water. We need water to survive. We likewise need Jesus, the Living Water to survive. Jesus told the Samaritan woman at the well that she would never thirst again if she partook of His Living Water. She was a social outcast because of her adulterous ways. The man she left back at the village while she drew water was not even her husband. Sex, drugs and lascivious living will not fill the void in our heart. That is reserved for only Christ. Holy Spirit is a gentleman. He knocks at the door of our hearts and waits until we invite Him in. He knocks but we have to answer the call.

1 Timothy 4:8 reads, "For bodily exercise profiteth little: but godliness is profitable unto all things, having promise of the life that now is, and of that which is to come." In my medical practice and through my community outreach I seek to strengthen and encourage the whole man. I often see patients who are out of balance. They either take great care of their physical bodies while neglecting their spirits and souls or vice versa. To accomplish all that the Lord has for us we must feed our bodies, souls and spirits. In the natural as in the spiritual realm what you feed will grow. We are instructed to worship God in spirit and in truth. We worship our God truly when we not only talk the talk but walk the walk. We worship Him in spirit and in truth when we do His will. Obedience is better than sacrifice. Actions speak louder than words ever will.

One of my mentors, Dr. Barry Cosper wrote this weekly newspaper article. It reads, "Study without service leads to spiritual stagnation. The old comparison between the Sea of Galilee and the Dead Sea is still true. Galilee is a lake full of life because it takes in water but also gives it out. In contrast, nothing lives in the Dead Sea because, with no outflow, the lake is stagnated. Can you see the logic of God's intent? If you want greater spiritual maturity and wisdom, you need to be pouring what you already know into the lives of others!" Jesus cursed a fig tree when it was not productive. We all have been given gifts and talents which we are to use for the Glory of God. We are to build His Kingdom on earth. His kingdom come, His will be done on earth as it is in heaven. As members of the Body of Christ we are kingdom builders under kingdom authority. We are to study to show ourselves approved. Faith without works is dead. Obedience is better than sacrifice. Benny Hinn writes in his book, *The Anointing*, "The presence of the Holy Spirit leads us to live in the power of the anointing if we are willing to pay the price of obedience."

We are triune beings: body, soul and spirit. We are created in God's image and are told to worship Him in spirit and in truth. The Trinity includes: God the Father, Jesus the Son and Holy Spirit. Jesus told the disciples that He must go but that He would leave them a Helper. That Helper who is also known as our Comforter is the Holy Spirit. We are saved by the grace and the gift of Jesus's Blood. We are redeemed back into relationship with a Holy God through our loving Savior. It is in Jesus's power that we are saved. Holy Spirit gives us God's enabling power to live a saved life in a sin filled world. The Holy Ghost communicates with us as believers who have accepted His presence spirit to spirit. Jimmy Evans explains in his book, *Ten Steps Toward Christ,* "The baptism in the Holy Spirit is about immersing us into an empowering relationship with the Holy Spirit so we can fully know and serve God. The Holy Spirit is God and is equal with God the Son and the Father. He always speaks and acts in accordance with the nature and Word of God. Thus, once we are saved and baptized in water, there is still another essential step we must take to be ready to live a successful Christian life—we must be baptized in the Holy Spirit. It is an experience subsequent to (after) salvation."

I was baptized by sprinkling as a baby in the Methodist tradition. I requested when I was a teenager to be submerged while visiting a Baptist church. It was as an outward confession of my inward beliefs. I met my Savior for myself. I accepting Jesus for myself. I then had a personal relationship with Christ for myself. We all have a choice to make and we all have an individual decision to accept or reject Jesus. Your mother and grandmother's salvation is not passed down nor promised to you. We all have to stand before our Maker. We have to decide of our own free will whether to accept Jesus as our Savior and Lord. It was years later that I received the Holy Spirit. I was visiting a church in my twenties which had several altar calls. I was raised to hear "the doors of the church are open": you would come up, join the church, and maybe accept Jesus as your personal Savior. This church offered a third option during their altar call for the Baptism of the Holy Ghost. I was well read on the subject but I had not experienced what I had read about. I wanted to take my walk with the Lord to the next level. I was in medical school and facing many challenges which I needed My Helper's Help. I walked the long aisle of this mega church and received the Baptism of the Holy Spirit with evidence of speaking in tongues.

The Word of God became alive and vibrant to me. It was no longer words on a page written years ago but it was pertinent and relevant to my life. Holy Spirit became my Counselor and Friend. As I spent time in His presence the clearer His Word became, both logos and rhema. I began hearing His voice through the words springing to life from the pages of my Bible. His still small voice also communicated Spirit to spirit with me. As I communed with Him, the clearer I heard His voice. Scripture says if you draw near to Him that He will draw near to you. I now crave times of silence and solitude so that I can listen to the Spirit of God's wisdom and revelation. Sheep know their shepherd's voice. He leads, guides and directs me in the will of the Father. Scripture instructs to pray without ceasing. I strive to be constantly in conversation with Holy Spirit. Prayer should not be a monologue but a dialogue. I talk and He talks. I listen and He listens. In the natural the more time you spend around a person the better you know their ways and their character. I know that God is a faithful and loving God because I have experienced His character. I know my Father's voice. Benny Hinn writes in his book, *The Anointing,* "First there must be the presence, and then comes the anointing. The anointing is not the baptism of the Holy Spirit, although that is important. The anointing is the power, the power to serve God. You will know assuredly when the presence of the Holy Spirit has come upon your life, for you will have sweet fellowship. And you will know immediately when He has empowered you ..."

Wisdom is discerning and following the Lord's lead for the various seasons of your life. True wisdom is hearkening to the voice of the Lord. Wisdom is going when He says go and staying when He says stay.

Wisdom is listening and yielding to the still small voice of the Holy Spirit even while your flesh is crying for vengeance or sensual pleasure. Proverbs tells us that wisdom is the principal thing and in all of our getting to get understanding. I was honored to be invited to speak the last two years in a row at a senior citizens health and wellness fair. It was held at the city's civic center. I encouraged the participants the previous year to "Finish Strong".

This year I encouraged the senior adults to share their knowledge and wisdom with the youth. I taught from the Book of Titus. My topic was the African proverb, "once you learn you teach". Once we as a people learn that our duty and purpose is to bestow our wisdom to the next generation then we teach. Each one should teach one because we truly stand on the shoulders of the generations before us. Don't let discomfort dictate or derail you from your destiny. For I am truly the hope and the dream of a slave. There is completeness through Christ.

I was taught as a youth that it is not what people call you but what you choose to answer to. It is not what people think of you but what God knows about you that is important. I struggled years with the responsibility of guarding my reputation against man's vicious assaults until I realized my only role is keeping my character. We are to keep our hands and hearts clean and God will protect our reputation. He is Our Keeper but we have to want to be kept. It often feels good to go off on a tirade and let emotions rule but one of the fruit of God's Spirit is self-control. He promises to fight our battles for us but we have to put down the weapons of vindictive words and actions. Scripture reminds us that the weapons of our warfare are not carnal but spiritual. The enemy might look flesh and blood but our real enemy is a spirit. We cannot be lulled into fighting each other because then we both lose. Evil can be wrapped in a beautiful package and vice versa. An ugly, tattered box can hold lovely contents.

My grandmother always said though that ugly is as ugly does. Judge a person by their actions and not by their outer appearance. What looks good is not always good for you. One of the kindest people that I have ever met could make a baby cry with his ornery looks. You should not judge a book or a person by its cover. Actions speak louder than words. A person can speak a thousand words and never say a word of truth. Watch and pray. In the words of my high school science teacher, Mrs. Bennett, "What does not come out in the wash will come out in the rinse."

Moses's mother placed him in the River Nile after the edict to kill the Israelite children was announced. Moses was discovered and drawn out of the water by Pharaoh's daughter. The enemy's plot was foiled by a baby once hidden in the water's weeds. As an adult, Moses led his people from captivity by parting the Red Sea with a rod. He used what was in his hand and what he had been taught to create a path of safety for his people. Moses' mother humbled herself and became the nursemaid for her own flesh and blood. She reared her son as she rocked him to sleep. Jochebed, Moses's mother taught him of their God and the struggles of their people. Moses knew who he was and whose he was despite being raised in Pharaoh's palace. Moses had a praying momma.

The Lord brought Joshua and the children of Israel into the Promised Land but scripture reminds us of a grim reality. The generation after Joshua died no longer knowing the God of their fathers. Judges 2:10 reads, "And also all that generation were gathered unto their fathers: and there arose another generation after them, which knew not the LORD, nor yet the works which he had done for Israel." It is our responsibility to train up our children in the ways of the Lord. We all have to make a living but we should also take the time to introduce our children to the Giver of Life. Don't allow the world's system, the Pharaoh of today, rear our children. Luke 18:16 reads, "But Jesus called them unto him, and said, Suffer not little children to come unto me, and forbid them not: for of such is the kingdom of God." There is completeness in Christ.

I often tell my patients who are successful in their careers that they should not only give their children a good secular education but to instruct them in the ways of the Lord. My foundation was rooted in the Word of God. My grandparents ensured that I was in Sunday school and church. When I went away to college I knew who I was and gravitated to the kids in the Campus Crusade for Christ. We owe our children this same firm foundation. Scripture reminds us in ALL of our getting to get understanding. We should not lose focus on Our Provider when the provision comes. We should not stop praying and Lord forbid not teach our children to pray when our prayers are answered.

Sunday mornings on my way to church I pass many parishioners washing their luxury cars in front of their beautiful homes. An idol is anything that we place above God. Exodus 20:2-3 reads, "I am the LORD thy God, which have brought thee out of the land of Egypt, out of the house of bondage. Thou shalt have no other gods before me." Jesus is the Chief Cornerstone. He is the foundation of our faith and our Rock. All other ground whether it be education or money is sinking sand. A person with an education without God is just an educated fool. A person with money without God is poor no matter the number of dollars in their bank account. Our Completeness is in Christ.

While writing this portion of the book I ran into a beautiful woman of God who shared her testimony with me. She lost her job because of medical problems. Her home which she shared with her disabled brother was about to be foreclosed upon. She said that she wrote seven letters to varying governmental and civic agencies for assistance. She said that she finally received a favorable response from the seventh letter. Her bills are now caught up. Her mortgage has been reduced nearly 200 dollars a month. She has a new job that is not as physically taxing. God is faithful but we must be steadfast. God will bless what we put our hand to. What if we are sitting back on our laurels and not putting our hands to anything? Are we giving God anything to bless? What area in our lives have we sat down on the promises of God? I encourage you to stand in your holiest of faith and start walking by faith and not by sight.

This woman was persistent in her requests for assistance. Her seventh request being the number of completion opened the door for her.

God holds the heart of the king in His hand and He turns it whichever way He desires. People who declined her 5th and 6th written pleas were made to review her requests again by a higher authority. Seven is the number of completion and wholeness. God makes us whole and complete not earthly riches or connections. Revelation 3:17-18 reads, "Because thou sayest, I am rich, and increased with goods, and have need of nothing; and knowest not that thou art wretched, and miserable, and poor, and blind, and naked: I counsel thee to buy of me gold tried in the fire, that thou mayest be rich; and white raiment, that thou mayest be clothed, and that the shame of thy nakedness do not appear; and anoint thine eyes with eyesalve, that thou mayest see." Trust God to make us rich in spirit and to renew our minds and lives. He opens the eyes of the blind. He is Our Provider. He is Jehovah Jireh and supplies all of our needs.

Proverbs 1:7 reads, "The fear of the LORD is the beginning of knowledge: but fools despise wisdom and instruction." I am not perfect. I make mistakes. God is not finished with me yet, but I try to retain a teachable spirit. It is hard to work or live with someone who thinks they know it all. We should seek to learn from constructive criticism rather than allow it to breed cynicism or contempt. The Book of Numbers tells the story of Balaam and his donkey. Balaam had made some unwise choices. The Lord allowed Balaam's donkey to try to speak some sense into him. If God opened the mouth of a donkey to try to save Balaam, who has He used to try to preserve you? We have heard the old saying, "don't shoot the messenger". Balaam threatened then beat his donkey three times. Scripture reminds us that it is hard to kick against the pricks. Often times we are placed in sticky or prickly situations that make us very uncomfortable.

It is our choice whether to learn the lesson or continue to go through the testing. I likened a young lady I was counselling to the children of

Israel being delivered from Egypt. She was recently freed from the hold of an abusive relationship but because of loneliness she was making some unwise choices. This young lady who knew the Lord was dabbling on lesbian dating sites. I explained to her that God's chosen people complained after being delivered of hunger while eating manna from heaven. They longed for the food they had in Egypt. They forgot their meals were soaked with the tears of bondage. I encouraged her to find her freedom in Christ. He is the only One that can fill the void she was feeling.

Balaam tried to run from the word of the Lord. The donkey he fled on became a messenger from the Lord. Jonah tried to escape from his calling. A whale held him captive until he stopped resisting. What are you allowing to hold you captive? What old habits are you allowing to keep you trapped in your past? You can't outrun God. Scripture reminds us that we have heavenly treasures in earthen vessels. We are the salt of the earth. If salt loses its flavor it is good for nothing. Many of us are scarred, marred and broken because we keep kicking against the pricks. We break our bodies down with drugs, alcohol and illicit behaviors but we expect our vessel to be intact. A broken vessel oozes its treasure. Only whole-heartedly accepting Jesus can make us whole again. Colossians 1:17 NIV reads, "He is before all things, and in him all things hold together."

Jesus is the only way to be made whole or complete. Many of us fight the process. We often try to drown out His sweet voice by turning up the noise in our lives. We attempt to create a distraction with unhealthy relationships, pursuing worldly riches and fame. You cannot exclude the Creator from His creation. We were made in His image to be in relationship with Him. Jesus is the only person who will ever complete us. We may try to find worldly pleasures that compete but they will not complete us. We were created for His Glory. There is a special assignment or calling on each of our lives. Some assignments are smaller than others but they are all important to the Body of Christ, as a whole. I illustrated this point in a recent speaking engagement. I told the ladies in attendance an analogy of a puzzle. If a 1,000 piece puzzle was only missing one piece it would still be incomplete. Are you the missing piece in your local church? Is the absence of your gift or talent hindering progression? Many of us understand this concept well but we still choose not to share our God given abilities. Lester Sumrall explains in his book *The Gifts and Ministries of the Holy Spirit,* "Spiritual gifts are not the icing on the cake or the meringue on the pie; they are the weapons of our warfare. The gifts of the Spirit are not designed just to make you different from other people. They are given to equip you for God's service." The motto of my home church, Mount Pilgrim Baptist Church is that we are a people building ministry building people for the Kingdom of God. We all have been given unique and useful gifts by the Giver of Life. We are to show His light to a dark and dying world. Speak life. Show love and give God the glory.

Because of pride and the desire for recognition some of us inwardly want people to fail or maybe just flail a little. We want them to recognize our importance. This ungodly mindset can be seen in businesses, churches and relationships. Our growth and wholeness is achieved by appreciating that Christ is the giver of our gifts. James 1:17 reads, "Every good gift and every perfect gift is from above, and cometh down from the Father of lights, with whom is no variableness, neither shadow of turning."

Our salvation is through His grace and not by our works or achievements. We have no need to compare or compete. We are all different but we are all needed in varying capacities. Scripture reminds us that our ears don't complain that they are not eyes. They just function in their assigned role. Your gift will make room for you but you have to walk in faith and not by sight. Don't get caught up by who you see achieving and reaching goals faster than you. My mother always said not to wish for something someone else has. You don't know how they got it or what they have to do to keep it. What God has for you is for you. Don't have a crab in a barrel mentality. We stand on the shoulders of the ones before us. Have big enough shoulders to bolster someone else up. I praise God for my mentors. He has given me godly men and women to speak life and wisdom to me. I try to continue the tradition of the African proverb, "Once you learn, you teach". So, I have mentored many students striving for careers in medicine. Scripture says that in a multitude of counsellors there is wisdom.

We can have great idea after great idea, but if we never put our ideas into action then we are merely dreamers and not achievers. We have to put action behind our passion for our dreams to come into fruition. God gives vision and provision but we must push past self-imposed or socially imposed limits. The Lord holds the heart of the king in the palm of his hand and turns it whichever way He desires. I have seen with my own eyes that scripture is true and God is faithful. Favor does not come from the East or the West but from the Lord. The national news reported in 2016 that the East and West side schools were ruled to integrate in Cleveland, Mississippi. These two schools and communities were historically separated by the now-abandoned Illinois Central railroad track. This decree occurred sixty-two years after the landmark Topeka vs. the Board of Education ruling. I pose the question, is justice delayed, denied? Locals point out to CNN that, "the specter of institutional racism looms over the schools' demographics." The first African-American Valedictorian of the predominately Caucasian West Side High was not until 2016.

I left an established and thriving medical practice on the West side with clean hands. I sought a fresh start on the East side due to dirty dealings by polluted people and institutionalized corruption. I soon saw that it does not matter what side of the tracks you are on. There are good and bad people everywhere but God's favor has no boundaries. Within six months God showed His faithfulness and gave increase of my medical practice. He expanded my territory with community outreach North, South, East and West.

I was asked why I still held health and wellness events on the West side. This is similar to asking why water is wet or why a caged bird still sings. We are created for a reason and for a season. A bird sings because that is intrinsically what it is. A person's physical body can be bound but its spirit is still free. I know why the caged bird sings. It sings for you and me. It sings to remind us to never let any opposition or persecution silence our voices. Our words have power but only if we utilize them. We must *Lift Every Voice and Sing.* Don't let anyone silence who you are. Never forget that who the Son sets free is free indeed. We are now free from the bondages of the doctrine of man and their limitations and stereotypes.

Patients over the years have expressed their confidence and comfort with my care. Many disenfranchised sick, poor and minority patients have confided that other physicians, "would not even touch me." They were made to feel less than human by their doctors because the ones caring for them would not even touch them during their physical exams. One of my one-hundred year old patients who was born into share-cropping and lived through segregation encouraged me with the following words. She said, "I like coming to your office cause you treat everybody the same. You are kind, laugh and talk to everyone—black, white, old, young, rich and poor. Don't change." Mark 15:15 reads, "And he said unto them, Go ye into all the world, and preach the gospel to every creature."

Maya Angelou writes in her epic poem, *I Know Why the Caged Bird Sings:* "The caged bird sings with A fearful trill of things unknown But longed for still and his Tune is heard on the distant hill For the caged bird sings of freedom." We are the hope, the dream and the delayed destiny of a slave. That is why the caged bird sings. It sings of freedom. Its body might be locked behind bars but its song can be heard for miles in the distance. Don't just appreciate your freedom of speech but let your voice be heard. Each one Teach one. Offer a hand up so we all can walk with our heads held up. Keys to success are never forgetting where you came from and always reaching back to give a helping hand.

Every key is cut to fit only a certain lock. There is a problem that you were intricately and specifically designed to solve. You are not here by accident but made for a unique reason. I urge you to unlock your potential and seek your purpose. Your Maker placed that passion on the inside of you. It is your job to discover it. Our success is not in our looks or long flowing locks. Samson thought the key to his strength was his hair. Truly it was in the covenant with His Father. Our God is faithful to keep a promise even if we are not strong enough to keep our end of the bargain. God is the true promise keeper. Samson revealed his secret to his lover, Delilah and she betrayed his trust. She arranged for him to be captured after she cut his hair. Samson had taken the Nazarene oath which included never to allow a razor to touch his head. Samson was shaven and betrayed by the prostitute, Delilah. He was literally blinded by lust. His captors gorged out his eyes and placed him in shackles. Despite Samson's physical weakness, God still showed Himself strong. Blind, bald and weakened, God restored Samson's strength and he defeated the enemy. God is faithful and the source of our strength. Power, position and people will fail you but God never fails. He is faithful to do what He said He would do. He is a Promise Keeper and we are complete in Him.

I can only educate one patient at a time, within the confines of my exam room walls. But, I was blessed to minister to about 1,500 people at one time at a single event held at a western area civic center. Jabez prayed for God to enlarge his territory and Isaiah 54:2 instructs, "Enlarge the place of thy tent, and let them stretch forth the curtains of thine habitations: spare not, lengthen thy cords, and strengthen thy stakes." We are directed to enlarge our tents in preparation for the increase and to stretch and strengthen our talents. We must prepare for the increase. We must study to show ourselves approved and lean not on our own understanding. The ways that seem right to a man such as forsaken and forgetting from whence you came lead to failure.

When God's face shines upon you no one nor nothing can infiltrate that light with darkness. Moses's face literally glowed after being in God's presence. Allow the Light of the World to radiate His love into your dark and gloomy situations. Our God is limitless but our faith is often limited by what we see. We are instructed to walk by faith and not by sight. Look past what your parents did or did not achieve and see the Hope of Glory. Look past the boundaries and glass ceiling that man has tried to limit you with and see the God who parted the Red Sea. No barrier nor wall can limit God's word and work. The question is what side of the sea are you standing? I had a vision a few years ago of the ocean rolling and retreating back and forth on the seashore. A line was being drawn in the sand. The line has been drawn spiritually and in the natural realm. It is your choice whether to be found in faith or in the waters of the flood.

Joseph was a dreamer but he was diligent in the things of his lord. He was blessed whether in Potiphar's house or in prison. His own brothers sold him into slavery. Joseph's brothers did not sell him because of the coat of many colors. They betrayed their baby brother because they were green with envy. The spirit of jealousy is vile and loathsome. It has made many envious people contemplate and commit great atrocities. No matter the plots and plans of the enemy God's people will prosper. Genesis 39:3 reads, "And his master saw that the Lord was with him, and that the Lord made all that he did to prosper in his hand." Maya Angelou writes in her poem, *Still I Rise,* "Out of the guts of history's shame I rise Up from a past that's rooted in pain I rise I'm a black ocean, leaping and wide, Welling and swelling I bear in the tide. Leaving behind nights of terror and fear I rise Into a daybreak that's wondrously clear I rise Bringing the gifts that my ancestors gave, I am the dream and the hope of the slave. I rise"

Love God and do good and things will work out for your good. Haters are going to do what they do, which is to hate. We must rise above the hatred and animosity, love God, do good and pray for those who despitefully use us. Joseph called for his brothers during the time of famine. He did not beckon them to the castle to boast or gloat. He blessed the ones who had thrown him in a pit as a young lad. Romans 12:20 reads, "Therefore if thine enemy hunger, feed him; if he thirst, give him drink: for in so doing thou shalt heap coals of fire on his head."

Oftentimes enemies are those we hold close to our bosom. A snake can only bite you if it is within striking distance but remember God is your shield. We are instructed in scripture to put on the whole armor of God so we can resist the enemy. Serpents not only slither but walk amongst us each day. They are in the hearts of evil men. I have wasted countless hours devising defenses against accusations and assaults. The stones were often hurled many times by those close to me. I've learned to trust God. My Sunday school teacher, Deacon Donald Talley often reminds us to rise above the snake line. There is reportedly a mountainous elevation that does not support the survival of these venomous creatures.

We must seek to continue to rise above small minded people. They are attempting to pull us down in the mud. Imagine if one person pulled another into the mud with them and they began to wrestle. A passer-by who did not see the initial assault will just see two dirty people in the mud. Our focus should be on keeping our hands clean and our hearts pure. Allow God to fight your battles. Don't get pulled into petty brawls. We rise to higher spiritual heights during worship. I often get a clearer, bird's eye view when I am in a position of worship. Hot cars can't run and hot heads can't think logically. Jesus instructs us to not only forgive our enemies seven times but seventy times seventy. Unforgiveness and bitterness can cloud your thinking. I've heard people say that they were so angry that they could not think straight.

God is love and love is patient and kind. This does not mean we are to be doormats. On the contrary, scripture says that when people do not receive your words to shake the dust off your feet when you depart. We can show love at a distance. You can forgive and still not restore a person to a place of fellowship. Don't hold a snake in your bosom unless you want to be bitten. Once a person displays his intentions and true nature believe what you see. Stop defending and denying and stop remaining in dangerous and potentially damaging relationships. Warning comes before destruction.

I have been honored to be a guest on Mr. Ron January's of Birmingham, Alabama radio program, Open Mic, several times over the years. We have discussed everything from health care and disease disparity in African Americans to spiritual and physical wellness. One of the shows long time caller's sign on is, "I'm just a voice crying out in the wilderness." Warning comes before destruction. Someone has to open their mouths and warn or we are all headed for destruction. Our people perish for the lack of knowledge. It is our role to warn but it is a person's choice to heed the warning. Isaiah 40:3-5 reads, "The voice of him that crieth in the wilderness, Prepare ye the way of the LORD, make straight in the desert a highway for our God. Every valley shall be exalted, and every mountain and hill shall be made low: and the crooked shall be made straight, and the rough places plain: And the glory of the LORD shall be revealed, and all flesh shall see it together: for the mouth of the LORD hath spoken it."

We must focus on removing bitterness, anger and unforgiveness out of our hearts. Bishop Roberto Jemmott expounds in his book, *Bishop's Pen*, "Suffering does not automatically make you stronger or better. What makes us stronger and better is the way we respond to suffering. If we respond by becoming bitter we fail to grow and we are not better. God provides us with His grace, but when I refuse that grace I create an environment where bitterness grows. I will either choose to forgive or dwell on the hurt, transgression or offense until I become bitter …

When you are bitter you become a slave to whom your bitterness is directed at." What you feed will grow. If you feed resentment, bitterness and anger then they will grow. Often the growth of these unhealthy emotions are beneath the surface. These unhealthy and unproductive emotions grow in the deep recesses of our heart. But, like an abscess, once it becomes toxic it inflames the surface and it then becomes noticeable to all. As a physician I have treated a lot of abscesses that often form because of a walled off cyst beneath the surface of the skin. If you only lance the surface of the skin the pressure is released but the infection can accumulate again. The core must be removed which is the root of the infection. The issues of life flow from the heart.

Man cannot curse what God has blessed and man cannot bless what God has cursed. But, God will not bless a mess. Several years ago, I was so excited to be joining a new practice. Unbeknownst to me the prior staff and physician were not eagerly anticipating my arrival. I looked differently than they did and my following of patients looked differently than them as well. I was still taking aback when the clinic director and physician called me in for a private meeting. I was told that if I did not play by their rules they would make me wither on the vine. I reported their discriminatory practices and derogatory statements. Glory to God, I have a thriving medical practice affiliated with another hospital system. The physician and director have found it difficult to maintain gainful employment. People will try to block your blessings but they will not succeed. We are the sons and daughters of Abraham and the blessing is upon us. I abide in Christ and He abides in me. John 15:5-6 reads, "I am the vine, ye are the branches: He that abideth in me, and I in him, the same bringeth forth much fruit: for without me ye can do nothing. If a man abide not in me, he is cast forth as a branch, and is withered; and men gather them, and cast them into the fire, and they are burned."

Seasons may come and go but God will get the Glory. God knows what is best for us and when we are mature enough to handle His blessing. Bishop Roberto Jemmott explains in his book, *Bishop's Pen: The Book,* "Life is governed by seasons. Since God operates in seasons, nothing happens in your life outside of seasons." We often have to go through a season of preparation to ready us for His best. A test often comes before God gives us His best. Joseph was lied on by a treacherous woman. His prison buddies forgot about him when they gained their freedom with Joseph's assistance. Joseph continued to stand for right and even when people did him wrong, Joseph stood with God. No matter how many people are against you if God is for you they cannot prevail. God will make your enemy your footstool and feed you in their presence.

Joseph continued to be about His Father's business whether in charge or in chains. God honored this steadfastness. Joseph had favor with God and man. God used Joseph to save his entire family in time of famine. Joseph went from prison to the palace. God will be glorified on earth as He is glorified in heaven. I praise Him for his miraculous and mighty acts. God is faithful to perform what He said He would do. One fruit of the Holy Spirit is long-suffering. Before a new road can be built a path has to be paved. Don't give up if things don't seem solid underfoot. Isaiah 28:16 reads, "Therefore thus says the Lord GOD: "Behold, I lay in Zion a stone for a foundation, a tried stone, a precious cornerstone, a sure foundation; whoever believes will not act hastily."

God still might be clearing some rocks and hindrances out of your way. I was about to start clinic a few days ago and I was led to go back in my office and pray. I saw in the spirit a big, rocky mountain but I felt that it would move by faith and by prayer. A few hours after interceding my daughter text me with good news about her college entrance exams. I was later notified that same day of my nomination for a city-wide honor. Upon returning home a letter was in my mail box regarding a state legislative investigation. They were reviewing the circumstances regarding the forged prescriptions in my name to hopefully prosecute the wrongdoers. Luke 18:7 reads, "And shall not

God avenge his own elect, which cry day and night unto him, though he bear long with them?" God is faithful and the prayers of the righteous avails much. We always triumph in Christ Jesus. Holy, Holy, Holy, Lord God Almighty. Worthy is the Lamb of God. Revelation 5:5 reminds us of God's faithfulness and our victory in Christ. It reads, "And one of the elders saith unto me, Weep not: behold, the Lion of the tribe of Judah, the Root of David, hath prevailed to open the book, and to loose the seven seals thereof."

Jesus is the beginning and the end. He knew us in our mother's womb. All through Christ: Christ through all. Christ in the good times and in the bad times. He sticks closer than any brother. He is a mother to the motherless. As the country singer croons, stop searching for, "love in all the wrong places" and learn to lean on God. He will not let you fall. Jesus holds all creation together. Trust Him with keeping the pieces of your life together no matter how broken you might feel. Jesus loves you and is calling you into a closer relationship with Him. He completes us. Bishop Roberto Jemmott also writes in his book, "I want to encourage you. It is not how your life story begins that matters, it's how you finish your story that counts. Finally, never be ashamed to share your story. If God delivered you from a life a sin, turn the page and never be ashamed to share it. Remember that you overcome by the word of your testimony." Jesus is the Word of God made flesh. He is the living embodiment of the Word of God. The Bible is the instruction manual of how to live the abundant life. Jesus is the way, the truth and the life. He walked this earth and led an unblemished life. He is the spotless, Lamb of God. He is God's perfect sacrifice and example of perfect love. Jesus's Blood that was shed on Calvary signifies the depth of God's love for mankind. For He so loved the world that He gave His Only Begotten Son. That is love. That is Jesus. Revelation 16:17 reads, "And the seventh angel poured out his vial into the air; and there came a great voice out of the temple of heaven, from the throne, saying, It is done." Jesus fights our battles and wins. He won the battle against sin, hell, death and the grave on the cross. Jesus gave up His spirit on Golgotha's Hill and said, "It is finished". The work is finished, done and completed in Christ's strength and power.

> **Joshua 6:4** *And seven priests shall bear before the ark seven trumpets of rams' horns: and the seventh day ye shall compass the city seven times, and the priests shall blow with the trumpets.*

# NOTES

# SUMMARY

Easter Sunday about five years ago I was awakened by the Holy Spirit and led to pray. During that early morning time of meditation the Lord revealed many truths about my calling and purpose. My Heavenly Father ministered to my spirit. I heard among other things that He was giving me a platform to utilize my medical degree because people respected degrees. He explained that He gave me this degree for His glory. I then heard the word mantle. A mantle represents spiritual authority or anointing. The Prophet, Elijah passed his mantle to his student and protégé Elisha. I heard that I would write books. This was years prior to me putting pen to paper for *Fountain in the Valley*. Many other details of my destiny were given while I basked in the presence of the Lord.

I then saw in the spirit, the face of one of my high school classmates. I had not seen him in over twenty years. This had previously happened while in prayer and since then. Usually it means that I am supposed to intercede for that person but sometimes the Lord has a message for him/her that I am supposed to share. I prayed and the heaviness in my spirit persisted. My prayer burden did not lift. I recognized that a message needed to be delivered to my former classmate. I promised the Lord that if He told me what to say and showed me how to contact the person that I would. I was led to open my Bible. I had written the following words on a sticky note a few weeks ago and placed them in my Bible. The note still is in my Bible. It reads, "I am your first love. I am the lover of your soul. I am calling you higher in me. You hear me. You know my voice. You know my ways and your ways are not my ways. If my people will turn from their evil ways then they will hear from heaven. TURN." I saw in the spirit who to call and I now knew what to say. Remember, I have not seen nor talked to this person in over twenty years and it was early, Easter morning. Obedience is better than sacrifice. I asked Holy Spirit how to contact this person and to open the doors of communication. Within ten minutes I had the phone number but I had to gather the gumption to dial it. James 1:25 reads, "But whoso looketh into the perfect law of liberty, and continueth therein, he being not a forgetful hearer, but a doer of the work, this man shall be blessed in his deed."

My classmate sleepily answered the phone, "Hello". I had to explain and make him remember who I was. The Valedictorian of your high school class, etc … He said, "Oh, yeah", but that still did not explain why I was calling him after all these years at this time of the morning. I explained my dilemma. I nervously continued that I was praying and the Lord placed him in my spirit. I told him that I had a message to give him. I read it and he said, "I know". We hung up the phone. My part was done. I watered the seed in his heart.

Delayed obedience is still disobedience. We must be punctual in the things of our Lord. There is a season for everything even for our words. God prepares the ground for the seed. He prepares the person's heart for His word that He wants you to plant. Our job is to be obedient. My spirit was vexed a few years ago because someone near and dear to my heart had not accepted the Lord. I prayed and I fasted. Any word the Lord placed on my heart I shared with my loved one. I confided this burden to my Pastor, Dr. David Craig. He reminded me that my job was to plant, another person's was to water but God will get the increase. Our job is to be obedient to the Spirit of the Lord. We all have free will, though. As Bishop Jim Lowe says, "life is choice driven and you live or you die by the choices you make."

This was not the first uncomfortable message that I had to track down one of my classmates to give. Interestingly, this particular word was for someone whom I had a somewhat contentious relationship with as a teenager. I searched and found her contact information and shared a similar word as above. Her response was humorous at the least and offensive at the most. She told me, "God spoke to Balaam through a donkey so I guess He can use you, too." My part was done. The seed was planted. Someone else will water but God will get the increase.

The Lord has been opening many doors for me to minister at churches. I mainly teach about health or wellness or through my books. On one such occasion I taught on not casting stones when you live in glass houses. I spoke from the story of the woman who was caught in adultery but Jesus stood up for her. Jesus did not permit her to be stoned. I tied in the story of Stephen who was the first recorded deacon. Scripture says that while Stephen was being stoned by the Sanhedrin counsel for his belief in God, he saw Jesus standing at the right hand of God. I encouraged the church that if Jesus stood up for them that He will stand up for them, too.

I was startled when the pastor of the church's secretary tapped me on my shoulder after I finished speaking. She said that the pastor wanted to see me immediately in his office. I knew that I had said what the Lord had laid on my heart to say to the congregation. I had never been to this church before and I knew none of their in-house issues. I did confide my topic to my husband the evening before and he remarked that he did not know if I was going to get invited back there again, with the topic of adultery. Obedience is better than sacrifice but it did not make the walk to the "principal's office"/pastor's study any easier. To my surprise, the pastor thanked the Lord for sending a prophet to his congregation. He said that I was a gift to the Body of Christ. I praise God for sending me and giving me a mantle to spread His Word.

I was asked to speak at a health and wellness conference at another church. I discussed both physical and spiritual health. I shared the story that is included in this book about a young lady with brittle bone disease. She continues to work for the Lord from a wheelchair. I reminded the members of the congregation that their body is the temple of the Holy Ghost. They were told that they need to be good stewards of their bodies by getting regular physical exams, exercising, eating healthy and not smoking. I was led to keep repeating the term, "No Excuses" during my presentation. Afterward the pastor's wife tearfully took the microphone. She reminded the attendees that, "No Excuses", was the word that her husband had given the congregation at the beginning of the year. He told them that there were no excuses for forsaking the assembly. He also emphasized that there were no excuses for not utilizing their gifts and talents for the glory of God.

One of the most challenging assignments that I have experienced was speaking at a leadership conference at my home church. I knew many things in the natural. I had a hard time teasing out fleshly knowledge from spiritual wisdom. It is easier for me to speak to a group of people that I do not know anything about. I am then depending solely on the guidance of Holy Spirit rather than soulish sources. We are directed not to lean on our own understanding but to acknowledge God in All of our ways. Challenging situations allow opportunities for God to stretch us. If we never face difficulties, we don't grow. The pearl is my birth stone and this opulent stone is formed when an irritant enters an oyster's shell. Beauty is often born through pain.

As a physician I have been privileged to deliver nearly one hundred babies. The end result of a new life entering the world is beautiful but the process is painful. The birthing process of All *through Christ: Christ through All* was painful but I pray you find it beautiful.

There are three recognized stages of childbirth. In the first stage a woman's body prepares for the delivery of the baby. The cervix dilates to allow room for the infant's entry into the world. In the spiritual realm likewise there is a preparation stage. If this stage is rushed spiritually or naturally you can be harmed. Anyone who has been in the delivery room knows that the doctor measures the dilation of cervix repeatedly. The mother is having very painful contractions during this stage of delivery but she CANNOT push against a closed cervix. It can cause damage to her. The baby's head contraction after contraction presses against the cervix and gradually it dilates. The magical diameter of ten centimeters is eventually reached. God also prepares us during our sometimes painful process of delivering our promise. I want to encourage you today not to give up on God. Don't give up on what He has promised to perform through you. God is faithful to do what He said He would do.

The second stage of delivery is the actual birth of the baby. It is a dangerous time. Many things can go wrong. I would have to check for and remove if needed a nuchal cord. That is when the umbilical cord is dangerously wrapped around the baby's neck. When this was felt or detected, I would have to ask the weary mother to stop pushing. If not, the infant could become strangled. I warn you readers not to kill your own dream by limiting yourself or by placing limits on God. I heard a radio personality say recently that small minded people cannot handle your big dreams. Don't let another person's insecurities and doubt kill your dream.

The third stage of delivery is the afterbirth. Early in our training we were only allowed to practice for upcoming deliveries by delivering the placenta or the afterbirth. After our dreams have come true and our purpose is birth don't forget about the afterbirth. The placenta functions to nourish the baby in the womb. Its purpose is beautiful but it sure is ugly. Success will sometimes uncover ugly flaws and frailties in our own character. These imperfections need to be dealt with before another seed can be sown and nurtured to maturity. The placenta needs to be removed or infection can develop. This infection can damage the womb thus preventing further pregnancies. Galatians 5:1 reads, "Stand fast therefore in the liberty wherewith Christ hath made us free, and be not entangled again with the yoke of bondage."

God is faithful. He sends but He will not send you unprepared. He promises not to make you ashamed. The people that you meet and the connections that you make are not coincidental. God is the Potter and we are the clay. He is constantly molding and making us into His image. Our job is to submit and remain pliable. We need to try to retain a teachable spirit and an open heart. No matter who has hurt us or what disappointments that we have experienced we should seek to guard our hearts. Bitterness, anger and resentment can harden our hearts and limit our malleability. Malleability plus availability equals usability. Never be too busy for God. Most of the divine revelations that the Lord has shown me have been while I was still. My mind was quiet and my heart was open to receive. Be still and know that He is God. The Holy Spirit is a gentleman and speaks in a still, calm voice. He is speaking to us but often we are too preoccupied to hear Him. Be still and know that He is God. Listen, watch and pray.

Bishop Darryl Jackson in one of our Remedy classes reminded us to see all situations through Jesus. Bishop Jackson taught us from Hebrews 2:9 which reads, "But we see Jesus, who made a little lower than the angels for suffering of death, crowned with glory and honour; that he by the grace of God should taste death for every man." We should train our eyes to see Jesus in the good and in the bad. Scripture teaches us to think on those things that are lovely and true. Jesus is truly working it all out for our good. I was blessed to care for a young lady who was recovering from a debilitating illness. She was hospitalized for months and had to even relearn how to walk. She tearfully said that she now truly sees the green grass and blue skies. The beauty was there before her illness but she did not take the time to see what was right before her eyes. She admitted to taking so many things and people for granted. We were all once blind but only by God's grace we now see.

I was sitting on my bed meditating when I saw the vision for the cover of *All Through Christ: Christ Through All*. I did not know then that this vision was to be a book cover. I saw a flag in the spirit realm. I have an undergraduate degree in Biology and I even considered majoring in meteorology for a while rather than medicine. God knows our predilections. He made us so He knows that I would notice that the flag in the vision was pointed toward the West. A storm was blowing the flag out of its usual position. As I looked closer and prayed harder I saw images on the flag. They were all symbols of God's protection. I saw the Lion of Judah, a dove representing Holy Spirit, and the Lamb of God. There was also rainbow that symbolized the covenant relationship that God spoke to Noah. The flag pole had an eagle at the top. God gives us the strength to mount up on the wings of eagles.

The significance of the flag is that God is Jehovah- Nissi. He is the Lord God Our Banner. He goes before us and protects us. He is Our Shield and Our Banner. We can do all things though Christ. He will be with us to cover us on sunny or stormy days. He is not a fair weather friend. He is the friend that sticks closer than any brother. God is faithful to do what He said He would do. We can do all things through Christ that strengthens us. Jesus cares for us and He takes care of us. I was speaking at a before mentioned Mother's Day tea from 1 Corinthians 13:13 ESV. The scripture reads, "So now faith, hope, and love abide, these thee three; but the greatest of these is love." I was unaware that an artist was in the audience whose newest painting was entitled, "Faith, Hope, Love".

I asked my daughter to come up and assist me as I made a flower arrangement in a vase with the word love painted on it. I described to the gathering how The Lilly of the Valley and the Rose of Sharon were symbols of Jesus. A Rose of Sharon thrives in deserts. I encouraged the group that Jesus will be with us in the parched dry seasons of our life or in our deserts. He is also our Lilly of the Valley. My teenage daughter arranged the beautiful roses and lilies in the vase. I told the crowd that a picture is worth a thousand words as we presented the flower arrangement to my mother. Love is what love does. A young artist who was attending the tea with her mother approached me afterwards. She said my talk encouraged her. She felt the Holy Spirit was ministering to her when I said, "a picture is worth a thousand words." She later blessed me with a copy of her painting, "Faith, Hope, Love." This talented woman painted the cover for *All through Christ: Christ through All*. All things do work together for those who love the Lord and are called for His purposes.

The events of the Resurrection morning, before mentioned, tied into the vision of the flag. I heard five years prior that Easter Sunday that the higher I lifted the Lord the bigger God's shadow covering me would become. The vision of the flag was the visual depiction of His words some years prior. As we lift the Savior up, He will draw all men toward us. He expands our territory and He likewise enlarges our covering. Jehovah Nissi covers me and my family. He keeps us safe even in the storm. Psalm 91:1 reads, "He that dwelleth in the secret place of the most High shall abide under the shadow of the Almighty." God was showing me in the vision the secret place of the Most High. He was encouraging me that if I dwell in His secret place that He will keep me safe. God is a Keeper and He is faithful. I have shared the tumultuous events of the last few years of my life in this book. I can truly say at the end of it that God was with me through it all. I know without a shadow of a doubt that I am in the shadow of the Almighty. Be encouraged that we can do all things through Christ that strengthens us. Thank you for going on the journey of *All through Christ: Christ through All* with me.

# Let Go and Let God

Let Go and Let God
It's a new season
Old things have passed away
Walk into your future
Without memories of past mistakes
Decide to let go of yesterday's failures
Make room for the success of today
Seek to seize tomorrow's victories
While the window of opportunity is opened by grace
Many can't grab hold of their dreams
Because
Their hands are full of fear
Many of our shoulders
Are
Still bound by the shame of yesteryear


Let Go and Let God
Jesus washed us white as snow
When His crimson Blood flowed down Golgotha's hill
Let Go and Let God
His nail
Pierced hands and arms stretched wide
Shows the depth and width of His love
He is beckoning us to cast our cares upon Him
Let Go and Let God
Each thorn in the crown bore our shame
He cares for us and this will never change

The chastisement of our peace was upon His head
Let Go and Let God
His grace is sufficient
His strength is made perfect in our weakness
Let Go and Let God

# WORKS CITED

Adam, Adolphe. "O Holy Night". 1847

Ames, Joni. (2014-2016). Classes conducted from King's Way Church, Irondale, Al and Church of the Firstborn, Cottondale, Al.

Angelou, Maya. (1994).The Complete Collected Poems of Maya Angelou. USA. Random House.

Bensinger,Tara. (2015). Deep Calling to Deep. A 33 Day Journey of Hearing God through His Word.

Brock, Joe. (2013-2015). School of the Prophets. Lectures conducted from Cutting Edge Ministries, Irondale, Alabama.

Cosper, Barry. (2016, January 13 and February 3). Just a Thought. *The Western Star,* p.5A.

Craig, David. (2016). Sermons conducted from Mount Pilgrim Baptist Church, Fairfield, Alabama.

Edwards, Gene. (1980, 1992). A Tale of Three Kings A Study in brokenness. Carol Stream, Illinois.Tyndale House Publishers, Inc.

Fuqua, Dennis. (2012). United and Ignited Encountering God through Dynamic Corporate Prayer.Vancouver, WA.USA.L/P Press.

Goll, James W. (2010). Deliverance from Darkness The Essential Guide to Defeating Demonic Strongholds and Oppression. Grand Rapids, MI. Chosen Books.

Goll, James W. (2007, April). The Prophetic Intercessor: Releasing God's Purpose to Change Lives and Influence Nations. Grand Rapids, MI. Chosen Books.

French, Bill and Michael. (2005). The Remedy Exercising God's Authority in Your Life. North

Sutton, New Hampshire. Streams Publishing House.

Hinn, Benny. (1992).The Anointing. Thomas Nelson Publishers. Nashville.

Holiday, Billie. "Strange Fruit" Fine and Mellow. (1939). Abl Meeroplol. Commodore.

Hughes, Langston. "Mother to Son" (1922). Retrieved March 4, 2016 from PoemHunter.com.

Jackson, Beverly. (2016). Sermons conducted from Church of The Firstborn, Cottondale, Alabama.

Jackson, Darryl. (2016). Lectures conducted from Advocate Ministries, Irondale, Alabama.

Jackson, Janet. "What Have You Done for me Lately?" Control. (1986) Jimmy Jam and Terry Lewis. Minneapolis.

Jackson, John Paul. Needless Casualties of War. (2009). Flower Mound, Texas. Streams Ministries.

Jakes, T.D. (2000, 2008). Life Overflowing Six Pillars for Abundant Living. Bloomington, Minnesota. Bethany House Publishers.

King, Martin L. Dr. Martin Luther King Jr. Quotations. Retrieved December 13, 2015, from www.drmartinluther kingjr.com.

King, Martin Luther. "I've Been to the Mountaintop". (April 3, 1968). Retrieved January 1, 2016, from American Rhetoric.com.

King, Martin Luther. "Letter from a Birmingham Jail". (August 1963). Retrieved January 22, 2016, from uscrossier.org.

Lowe, Jim. (2000-2002).Sermons conducted from Guiding Light Church, Birmingham, Alabama.

Macpherson, Sir William. "The Stephen Lawrence Inquiry". (February 1999) Retrieved February 25, 2016, from www.gov.uk.

Mariano, Willoughby. "How theft ring stole millions of drugs from Emory". The Atlanta Journal-Constitution. (March 10, 2016). Retrieved March 12, 2016.

McLaughlin, Eliott. "Mississippi town's views on desegregation ruling aren't so black and white". CNN.com (May 27, 2016).Retrieved June 2, 2016.

Newton, John. "Amazing Grace". (1779). Retrieved March 20, 2016, from Christianity.com.

Njoroge, Wanjiru Penny. "Healing Hope for your Grief and Bereavement". (2010). Bloomington, IN. Westbow Press.

Obama, Barak. "Remarks by the President in Eulogy for the Honorable Reverend Pinckney". (June 26, 2015). Retrieved January 23, 2016, from thewhitehouse.gov.

Obama, Barak. "Remarks by President Obama to the Kenyan People". (July 26, 2015). Retrieved February 1, 2016, from thewhitehouse.gov.

Omartian, Stormie. (1997). The Power Of A Praying Wife. Eugene, Oregon. Harvest House Publishers.

Parks, Rosa. (1994). Quiet Strength. Grand Rapids, Michigan. Zondervan Publishing House.

Sumrall, Lester. (1982). The Gifts and Ministries of the Holy Spirit. New Kensington, PA. Whitaker House.

Trimm, Cindy. (2010). The Art of War for Spiritual Battle. Lake Mary, Florida. Charisma House.

Warren, Rick. (2002). The Purpose Driven Life. Grand Rapids, Michigan. Zondervan.

Weir, David. (2016). Sermons conducted from Victory Christian Church. Pell City, Alabama.

Printed in the United States
By Bookmasters